D1279564

DOBBIE
DEFENDER of MALTA

Sir William, Lady Dobbie and their daughter at Gibraltar.

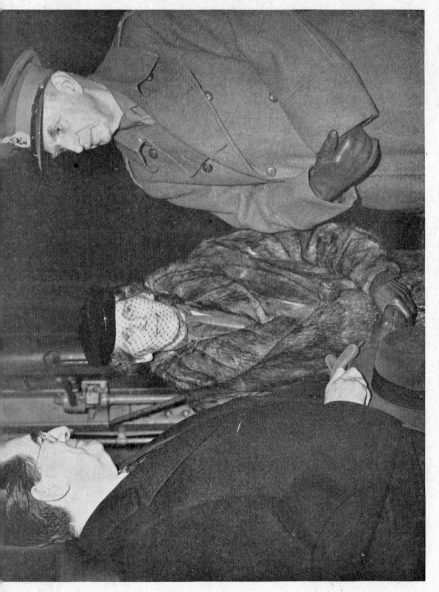

Dr. Houghton welcoming General and Lady Dobbie at New York.

DOBBIE
DEFENDER OF MALTA

by

S. Maxwell Coder

Member of the faculty, Moody Bible Institute

Published and Distributed by

Van Kampen Press

WHEATON, ILLINOIS

Printed in United States of America

DEDICATION

To my mother, whose prayers, teaching
and godly example brought me to the
Saviour she loved and served, this volume
is affectionately dedicated.

PREFACE

Every generation has its spiritually great. There is no occasion for us to say wistfully about a bygone age, "There were giants on the earth in those days!" All we need do is to look about us, and we find Christians who stand head and shoulders above common mortals, because of their absolute devotion to the Lord Jesus.

There are business folk, housewives, farmers, preachers, tradesmen, doctors, and representatives of almost every other walk of life, constantly revealing the sweetness and strength of Christ as they go about their daily tasks. It was inevitable that the second world war should bring into prominence many soldiers and sailors who took an uncompromising stand for the Lord. Of them all, Dobbie of Malta stands out as one of the most colorful, because of the peculiar circumstances in which his lot was cast.

For a surprising length of time he received world-wide attention as commander of the lonely garrison of a tiny isle which was bombed incessantly and with unprecedented ferocity. The press reports seemed always to mention his unswerving faith in God. Then, when Dobbie finally won through, instead of retiring into obscurity, he set forth as an ambassador of Christ. When he came to America, the unique spectacle of a famous governor-general turned evangelist aroused great interest in his meetings.

The general would be the last one to lay claim to unusual spiritual stature. Nevertheless, he has been so regarded by believers in two hemispheres, and thus there has come about a widespread hope that the story of his life might be made available for the Church at large. This book was written in the earnest conviction that the American ministry of Dobbie of Malta can be enlarged and bear still more fruit for the Lord Jesus Christ through this means.

God grant that American and Canadian soldiers especially, who had a part in the same war that sent the general to our shores, may find in this brief record of his life and ministry an incentive to devote their own lives to the Lord who revealed His hand at Malta and elsewhere. God still hears and answers the prayers of all who honor His Son as did the gracious Christian soldier who is described in these pages.

INTRODUCTION

Alexander Pope was not the first to declare that "The proper study of mankind is man." A much older version of the same idea is that expressed by Plato, "Trees and fields tell me nothing. Men are my teachers."

In the Bible, human life is often used for purposes of instruction. Some of its characters are good and become examples. Others are bad and are held before us by way of warning. But from all of them, we have something to learn.

In the volume to which this is your introduction, you are to meet face to face a man—and you can spell man with a capital M. The consideration of his varied and interesting life will yield dividends of pleasure and profit.

The author divides the story into three sections—The Man, The Mission, and The Message. The first section is biographical, naturally emphasizing the tremendous events at Malta.

The second section has to do with General Dobbie's American tour. That this was not a mere episode is evident from the fact that the General and his Lady in four and a half months covered approximately 15,000 miles in the United States and Canada, visited some 40 centers of population, and addressed approximately 150,000 people.

The third section is a further revelation of the man in the presentation of some of his utterances, spoken and written.

Frequently during the American tour, the writer of this Introduction was the person who at some luncheon gatherings had the privilege of presenting General Dobbie as the speaker. The chairman of the occasion introduced the introducer.

In this book I become a sort of chairman. Ladies and gentlemen, it is my privilege to introduce S. Maxwell Coder, member of the Faculty and Staff of the Moody Bible Institute, who will in turn present "Dobbie—Defender of Malta."

—WILL H. HOUGHTON

I
THE MAN

How God Prepared and Used His Servant

A STRIKING PARALLEL

THIS is the record of what God has wrought in the twentieth century through the apostolic faith of a man who met Christ, heard His Word, and was not disobedient to the heavenly vision. It is a story strangely parallel in its broad outlines to something which took place nineteen hundred years before.

In the providence of God, a chain of circumstances from ancient times is often found to be a type or prophecy of a series of events taking place long afterward as the divine program unfolds. "The thing that hath been, it is that which shall be; and that which is done is that which shall be done" (Eccl. 1:9). Thus it is with the account in Acts 28 of a tempest which brought the Apostle Paul to the island then called Melita, and the miracles that befell him there.

Certainly the beloved physician Luke had no thought that he was foreshadowing future events when he penned those lines about Paul and Publius, the first Christian governor of Malta. Yet when we read the familiar story again, in the light of what has occurred in recent times, we cannot help noticing a resemblance between two situations which stand at either end of nearly two thousand years of the island's long history.

Perhaps they are right who see portents of the nearness of the end of the present age in the prominence of Bible lands in world headlines today, after centuries of comparative obscurity. If so, there may be a significance in the incidents which we are about to relate beyond their unusual value as a contemporary record of the faithfulness of God to His written Word.

When first the tiny island of Malta appeared upon the

13

horizon of sacred history, a violent storm had overspread the Mediterranean Sea. Out of the storm emerged a scene of shipwreck. Forth from the shipwreck a man stepped upon the shore. Hardly had he arrived when a viper attacked and sought to destroy him. It came from a fire which "the barbarous people" had kindled. The man shook off the venomous beast and felt no harm. This so deeply impressed the people of that place, after they had looked a great while, that they acknowledged the hand of God had been revealed.

We turn from reading this in the Scripture to consider in outline the history of Malta during World War II. It centers in the experiences of a great Christian governor of that island, in whom are merged the characters of Paul and Publius. In the year 1940, the worst tempest of its kind ever known descended upon the Mediterranean. Dark war clouds hung low over the little island of Malta. When they broke, they precipitated a rain of fire from the sky. So fierce was the storm that it threatened shipwreck to the very civilization which had followed upon the preaching of the Apostle Paul.

For this hour of crisis, God had prepared His man of destiny. Forth from the tempest and the threatening shipwreck, stepped William George Sheddon Dobbie upon the shore of Malta. Scarcely had he arrived at the island when there came a viper from the fire which barbarians had kindled in Europe. It sought to destroy him, but he shook off the venomous beast, and felt no harm. In consequence, not only the people of that place, but the inhabitants of the whole world, having looked for a great while, saw a miracle wrought by faith alone, and realized that the hand of God had been revealed.

FIRST AND SECOND BIRTHS

This new Governor could never have carried with him

the eternal calm and strength which the Maltese had seen in Paul, had God not made him ready for the part he was to play in world events throughout a most unusual life. When he arrived at Malta in 1940, there were already 60 years of the providential movings of God in back of him. Ahead was a strange and violent pattern of events. Behind were the experiences by which the Lord had prepared His instrument.

From the very beginning, it seemed that Dobbie's destiny was to walk where other famous Christians had walked, and to sit where they sat. He was surrounded by an atmosphere of godliness from the day of his birth in Madras, India, July 12, 1879. His grandmother was a remarkable saint of God who had a wide influence on the British civil officials and army officers stationed in India. Even when she lay on her death bed, she called in each officer known to the family and spoke to each one about the Saviour's grace and love. Thus she spent the last three days of her earthly life.

The Christian testimony of the General's mother was no less notable and far reaching. In the midst of the American tour, at the close of a mass meeting in St. Louis, a clergyman of that city sought out Sir William and said, almost with tears in his eyes, "I must say to you how much I owe to your saintly mother. I was a missionary in India when she lived there. There came to me a time of tremendous doctrinal upset, when I faced the question of whether I should honor all of the Word of God and obey its every precept, no matter what the cost. At that great crisis in my Christian experience, your mother gave me the counsel and help I needed. To her I owe an everlasting debt of gratitude for encouraging me to follow God's Word wherever it might lead."

Sir William's father was W. H. Dobbie, Esq. He was better fitted by disposition for the Indian Civil Service than for the army, in which all of his brothers found their careers. He rose to occupy an important post in the finance department of that Service. At his retirement he was given the title of Companion of the Indian Empire (C.I.E.), an honor conferred upon distinguished military and civil servants of the Empire. During his years in India, although occupying a high social position, he and his wife were careful not to compromise their Christian testimony. They resolutely maintained separation from the gay life going on around them in which custom almost demanded that they participate.

There can be no doubt that the unusual conversion of his grandfather, an officer in the Indian army, exercised a strong influence upon the home into which Dobbie was born. There was a German missionary named Samuel Hebich working among the natives nearby. Finding a fertile field for evangelism among the young Europeans, he began to win them to Jesus Christ. One by one he buttonholed the officers of the regiment until each one was saved. Dobbie's grandfather told of how the tall ungainly figure of the missionary, under his green umbrella, came to where he was resting.

After a few minutes' conversation, Hebich said abruptly, "Get down the Book!"

The officer was too much startled to refuse. He took a Bible from the bookcase, the Book which formed a part of every officer's outfit, but which he had never even opened before.

"Read the first two verses of Genesis," said the man of God.

"In the beginning God created the heaven and the earth. And the earth was without form, and void; and darkness was upon the face of the deep. And the Spirit of God moved upon the face of the waters."

"That will do. Shut the Book, and let us pray."

The two men knelt together, while Hebich asked God to reveal to Dobbie his true condition in God's sight. Then the missionary departed. The next day he was back again.

"Open the Book and read the first two verses of Genesis."

Once more the officer complied. The prayer which followed had such an effect upon Dobbie that he remained under deep conviction of sin, seeing in himself an illustration of the words he had read. He realized that he was waste and void with the darkness of unconcern and unbelief upon him.

It was in this state of misery because of the reality of his sin that the missionary found the officer on the third day. Dobbie's heart was so full that he grasped the hand of his visitor and said:

"Mr. Hebich, I see it all. What must I do?"

"Read the third verse."

"And God said, Let there be light: and there was light."

"The Spirit of God has been moving upon your heart. God will give you light; believe on the Lord Jesus Christ and thou shalt be saved."

Hebich pointed the officer to the cross, and he entered into the experience of eternal life through faith in Christ.

The knowledge of salvation pervaded the very atmosphere of the Dobbie home from that time on. When the books are opened in heaven at last, that little known missionary will come up for remembrance. He had no small part in preparing the soil from which was to spring Dobbie of Malta, in the second generation. It is an interesting fact that this same individual led to Christ Lady Dobbie's uncle, who was likewise an officer of the Indian Army in that region.

There were no facilities for educating a child in the British tradition in India. One of the sacrifices required of those who engaged in either of the Indian services was early separation from their children. Dobbie's parents willingly made this sacrifice for his sake. When he was only nine months old, the opportunity was presented for a visit to England.

They brought him along, so that he might remain with relatives and friends on their return to Madras.

From the age of seven, the lad lived at a private boarding school, just one of a group commonly known as "the Indian children." It was not long before he exhibited a brilliance beyond his years, leading the class in Latin, Greek, and other classical subjects. When he was 13 years old, he took an examination for a scholarship at the Charterhouse school. Dobbie secured the highest grades in the class and won the appointment.

Charterhouse, although known as a public school in the English terminology, corresponds with the more exclusive private schools in the United States. It was opened at London in the year 1614, in a mansion originally used as a Carthusian monastery and later occupied by the dukes of Normandy as their home. About 1870, the school was moved out of London and rebuilt in the country some 35 miles away.

In entering Charterhouse, Dobbie was unconsciously walking in the steps of John Wesley. The Duke of Buckingham had nominated Wesley to the famous school in 1714. Both of the boys attained proficiency in the classical languages there. Both of them cherished a lifelong affection for the place.

Like John Wesley, Dobbie had a heart warming transaction with the Lord Jesus Christ by which the assurance of salvation came to him. It was as a boy of fourteen, one year after he entered Charterhouse, that he first came to know the meaning of the new birth. It was as definite and clear cut an experience as any other in the long and eventful years which followed.

Speaking to a gathering of young people in England half a century later, he recalled that first moment of the joy of new life through Christ, still undimmed with the passage of time. He said, "I always like to look back and remember the beginning of my Christian life, because without a beginning there is no life at all, and I look back to forty-nine years and more since by the infinite goodness of God I was brought to trust the Lord Jesus Christ as my Saviour. I was only a school boy at the time, about fourteen; and I felt the great burden of my sins. I thank God that He laid the burden upon me.

"Although I had heard the gospel over and over again, as you have, it had somehow not come home to me how that burden could be got rid of; but on the first Sunday in November, 1893, it suddenly came home to me what I had so often heard before, that the Lord Jesus Christ came into this world for the express purpose of giving His life so that He might bear, and pay the penalty of, my sins, so that I might go free.

"I had heard it often, but it had not come home to me before. I then, that night, accepted the Lord Jesus as my Saviour, my Companion, and my Lord—just by myself—there was nobody else in the room so far as I can remember; and from that day to this through all the ups and downs of Army life, I have never been able to doubt the reality of that transaction, and I know that then God for Christ's sake forgave me my many sins, and that on account of what Christ has done (and on that account alone) I go free. From that day to this the whole course of my life has been changed. I thank God more than I can say for that wonderful event in November, 1893."

MILITARY TRAINING

In the period immediately following his second birth, Dobbie sought wisdom from God in the choice of a career. In this he had the example of his parents, who had depended upon God's guidance throughout their Christian lives. He was convinced that God had a definite plan for him, into which he would be directed by prayer, God's Word, and providential circumstances.

It was quite natural that he should think of military service. For generations, most of his forebears had been army officers. His father was almost the only exception. In fact, it was some 800 years before, that the first soldier son of the Dobbie clan of Scotland went forth to battle in the Crusades. It was from Crusader ancestors that Sir William received his family crest, a simple but noble device known as the cross crosslets, formed by making the three upper arms of a Latin cross into small crosses by the addition of small transverse arms.

In the city of Edinburgh there hangs a silver arrow from which a silver shield is suspended. It dates back to the seventeenth century, when a company of Scots archers formed a bodyguard for the King. Every year a shooting match was held to encourage good archery. The silver arrow was awarded to the winner, and a medal was struck giving the name and heraldry of the successful contestant. Two such medals hanging in Edinburgh speak of the direct ancestors of Sir William, so far as can be discovered. The legend is engraved,

> "This arrowe has been winned three times
> by Capt. Robert Dobie of Stoniehill,
> 1641, 1642, 1645."

At the bottom appears the crest of the cross crosslets. In between, the likness of a man is to be seen upon the time-worn silver shield. His features bear a striking resemblance to those of General Dobbie. There has always been a Robert in the family. The General's grandson is named for this Scottish ancestor.

After carefully considering the teaching of the Scriptures about military service and concluding that it was perfectly consistent with the Christian life, Dobbie planned to make the Army his profession. The difficulty arose that one of his eyes did not come up to the required standard. However, he took the competitive examination at Charterhouse for admission to the Royal Military Academy at Woolwich, and through a series of circumstances in which he saw the hand of God definitely working, he was offered a place in the Academy, fulfilling his heart's desire.

Woolwich is the West Point of England. When Dobbie became a cadet there at the age of eighteen, he found himself among a group of young men just freed from the restraint of private school life. Most of them gave vent to their feelings by indulging in pleasure of every description. William joined himself to a small group of cadets who met regularly for prayer. They attended a Bible class taught by a gifted Presbyterian clergyman. The group became known among the other students as "The Pi Squad," from the Greek initial of the word "pious." Each was a marked man, subject to hazing, but the persecutions they endured for the sake of Christ became a source of spiritual strength to them.

Unlike Charterhouse, where Dobbie had been encouraged to specialize in classical languages, the Royal Military Academy of necessity emphasized mathematics in its curriculum. The young cadet found himself at a disadvantage in this one subject. He had to overcome the deficiency in his previous training, but soon found that he was now in his proper element. He possessed a gift for mathematics so remarkable that, starting from the bottom of the list of artillery students, he was able to climb forty places in one term. Had he remained another year in Woolwich, he might have been top man. As it was, he was numbered among the first dozen at his graduation. He secured the maximum grade in calculus.

From the Military Academy, William went on to the School of Military Engineering in Chatham. Despite the rigorous discipline of these years of training, he found time to engage in public witness for Christ. At Chatham there was a soldiers' home being run by a group of Christian ladies. He joined other students in going to the home to speak and conduct gospel services. All through his military career, Dobbie identified himself with the Officers' Christian Union, an organization of British officers determined to propagate the faith in every way possible. To him might be applied the immortal lines of Bunyan, "I have loved to hear my Lord spoken of, and wherever I have seen the print of His shoe in the earth, there have I coveted to set my foot also."

It was in military school that Dobbie first became interested in the battles and campaigns of the Old Testament. Some of these ancient records made such an impression upon him that in later life they supplied the key to his program for the defense of Malta.

In II Chronicles 20, he read of a situation faced by Jehoshaphat, the King of Judah, much like that which he was himself to face during World War II. Israel found herself attacked by three enemy nations. A great multitude from beyond the sea threatened the land and its capital city of Jerusalem. Three things are written about this godly king, which may likewise be written about the Governor of Malta. Jehoshaphat feared God; he set himself to seek the Lord personally; and he issued a public proclamation calling upon the people to ask help of the Lord in their extremity.

From the people of Israel the cry went up, "Behold . . . how they reward us, to come to cast us out of thy possession, which thou hast given us to inherit. O our God, wilt thou not judge them? for we have no might against this great company that cometh against us; neither know we what to do; but our eyes are upon thee."

From Jehovah came the answer, wonderfully fulfilled a second time in the Mediterranean nearly three thousand years later, "Thus saith the Lord unto you, Be not afraid nor dismayed by reason of this great multitude; for the battle is not yours, but God's. . . . Set yourselves, stand ye still, and see the salvation of the Lord." The would-be invaders were utterly confounded and brought down to defeat.

In 1899, Dobbie received his commission as second lieutenant in the Royal Engineers. It was the year in which the South African (Boer) War broke out. By 1901 he found himself engaged in that conflict, using his engineering skill in the building of blockhouses. In South Africa he won his first decoration, the Queens Medal with five clasps.

One of the young officer's first experiences of the practical value of faith in Christ came during the Boer War. He was taken with a severe case of typhoid fever followed by pneumonia. His condition became so serious that he was personally convinced he was dying. As he lay at death's door, God gave him perfect peace of mind. He knew that no earthly career could compare with the joy of being absent from the body and present with the Lord, if God should will it. He was entirely content with the prospect, although he was only 22 years old at the time. Recovery was accompanied by an abiding consciousness of the companionship of Christ.

MARRIAGE AND HOME LIFE

One of the notable milestones in Dobbie's career was reached in his marriage on April 7, 1904, to Sybil Orde Browne, sixth daughter of Captain Charles Orde Browne of the Royal Artillery. Perhaps no other event in his life gave greater evidence of the clear guidance and blessing of God than his marriage. He always insisted that any measure of success which attended his work was largely due to the inspiration and help he received from his wife. They were perfectly suited to each other in their social position, their tastes, and their Christian background.

Most important of these happy agreements was the fact that both young people were connected with the so-called Plymouth Brethren. In that intensively Biblical fellowship, they early came to know the Scriptures and to make the Bible their guide and the final court of appeal in everything.

Lady Dobbie's father came of a widely known Gloucestershire family which had always belonged to the Church of England. He was converted while a young officer in the horse artillery. After some persecution because of the stand he had taken, he decided to give up his promising career at the call of God to labor among the needy of Woolwich. There he built a mission hall (since destroyed by flying bombs), and he was instrumental in establishing an assembly of Plymouth Brethren. However, to the time of his death, he kept up his professional work by becoming a lecturer both to the Artillery and Naval Colleges on the armor plating of ships.

Like Sir William's, Lady Dobbie's family goes back to many generations of Army officers. Her brother was Major Granville Orde Browne of the Royal Artillery. Her nephew, a son of her eldest sister, was the world renowned General Orde Wingate of the Chindits, killed in action in Burma.

An unsuspected link with the future was forged in the Dobbie marriage. Lady Dobbie's father, while representing Great Britain as an expert in the design of ships' armor at the Chicago Exhibition of 1893, was taken through the Moody Bible Institute by D. L. Moody himself, and shown the work of the school which was to sponsor the General's tour of America in 1945.

Just a few months after beginning their life together, the couple went to Bermuda, where Dobbie served until 1907. They arrived in October; their first son was born one year later. It was during this period that they determined to establish and maintain a firm separation from the world. Everything was given up which they did not think would honor Christ. It was necessary to face the fact that such a stand was likely to affect their career. They agreed that if the young officer were ever given an assignment contrary to his Christian principles, he should resign so they could begin life again elsewhere. Only once did such a possibility appear on their horizon, but it was providentially averted.

In Bermuda they were stationed out in the country. The only Christian fellowship available was among the colored Brethren of the island, and so they regularly worshipped with these people. Dobbie found every true Christian grace exhibited by the members of the group, who were neither servile nor insolent. He found their attitude both dignified and respectful toward the only whites ever to enter their place of worship. Among them the officer met a man whom he described as one of the finest Christian gentlemen he had ever known, and with whom he corresponded for years. It was at one of the simple meetings conducted by their colored friends that Dobbie and his wife dedicated their first-born son to the Lord. This boy fell in Italy in 1944.

The years spent in Bermuda were important as a time for the laying of strong foundations. High courage was displayed in the way the young couple gave their clear testimony for Christ. They had no hesitation at posting notices of meetings on the telegraph poles along the roads, although such a thing was unheard of among British officers in that country. Separation from questionable amusements was maintained. Invitations received to young people's dances were firmly declined. Yet, so no impression of fanaticism might be created, they played tennis and engaged in every wholesome sport open to them on the island.

Profiting by this experience, Lady Dobbie always counseled young people who attended the large meetings she addressed in Britain and America, to take their stand against doubtful matters early in life. "The separated life is much easier then," she said, "than later. As the years pass, you will find your position becoming more difficult. If you should reach a position of prominence without such preparation, there is little likelihood that you will ever be able to deal with questionable situations in the Christian way."

As other children were born into the home, devotional customs were established and followed regularly, no matter where the officer was sent by his government. Each child was taught to offer prayers twice daily, on going to bed and on rising in the morning. The reading of Bible stories was never omitted. A family worship service was conducted on Sunday afternoon at three o'clock. One result of such determined maintaining of an altar in the household was that all three of the children came to know Christ in their own home. They voluntarily asked for baptism at the age of thirteen or fourteen.

Dividends from this investment of time and energy in spiritual things continued throughout the years for the General and his wife. They had peace of mind when their daughter Sybil was upon the submarine infested Mediterranean on her way to join them at Malta in 1940. They knew they had no reason to fear when their younger son, Major O. C. S. Dobbie, entered the war with the Royal Artillery. And when their older son, Major Arthur W. G. Dobbie of the Royal Engineers, was killed in action at Italy in June of 1944, they had the unspeakable comfort and assurance which God gives to all who put their faith in Him.

A British journal, in giving notice of the death of their son, said, "Major Dobbie followed in his father's footsteps spiritually, as well as in his brilliant discharge of his military duties; he was a keen member of the Officers' Christian Union, and took an active interest in the spiritual welfare of his men."

One example of the effect of consistent Christian teaching in the home stands out as an unusual demonstration of the power of the Word of God to mold the thinking and guide

the lives of children. After having heard a Bible story about
the patriarch Jacob, Arthur came in one day from the garden.
He remarked to his mother,

"I've just taken Jacob's vow about the tenth."

"What do you mean by that?" she asked him.

"Why, I built a little altar of stones out in our garden, like
he did at Bethel. Then I came in and asked the cook for
some oil. All she had was paraffine oil, but I took some and
poured it over the altar like Jacob did. Then I said, 'Of all
that Thou shalt give me, I will surely give the tenth to Thee'."

Lady Dobbie said nothing at the time, but when Sybil did
the same thing later on, and the youngest child followed the
example, she called them all together. Tactfully, she tried
to point out the seriousness of such a vow. She suggested
that they confess to God that they did not realize altogether
what they were doing, and ask Him to forgive them the
promise they might not be able to keep.

The children stoutly defended their action.

"We meant every word of it, mother," they declared.

"Remember, the Bible says, 'Better is it that thou shouldest
not vow, than that thou shouldest vow and not pay'," she
warned.

Each of them insisted that the promise would be kept con-
scientiously. So careful were they about the tithe, in fact,
that their parents were in turn brought to a more perfect
regard for the principle themselves.

Shortly after, Sybil came in with the announcement that
she had given a half-crown to a beggar whom she felt to be
undeserving.

"But, mother, I shall not take the money from my tithe.
I realize that I probably should not have helped the man, but
I did it anyhow, in spite of my better judgment, and so I paid
it out of my own money."

That same afternoon Sybil picked up a half-crown from

the floor of a room where some ladies had been meeting. Everyone disclaimed ownership of the coin. It was left in her keeping until its owner should inquire after it. As they left the place, she said to her mother, "Do you know, I think we shall never hear any more about this. I believe the Lord has repaid me the money I gave to the beggar." And so it turned out.

Everyone who knew the General and his wife, was aware of their deep affection for each other. They could not have concealed it, even had they desired to do so. They beautifully exemplified the teaching of the Scriptures as to the ordering of a Christian household. Lady Dobbie accorded to her husband the place of headship; Sir William always gave to his wife the place of honor; and the children were happy to be in their place of obedience.

The words written by the General upon the flyleaf of a Bible treasured by his wife as a gift from him epitomized as well as anything could the basis upon which they builded their lives and the mutual esteem they held for each other. There were two Scripture references, with a Bible phrase written beneath.

"The Lord is my light and my salvation; whom shall I fear? The Lord is the strength of my life; of whom shall I be afraid?"   (Psalm 27:1)

"And the Lord shall guide thee continually, and satisfy thy soul in drought, and make fat thy bones: and thou shalt be like a watered garden, and like a spring of water, whose waters fail not."   (Isa. 58:11)

"They went both of them together."

The world knows today how God has honored these two who made Him their light, their salvation, and the strength of their life. The reward He has given publicly to His servants for their secret prayer and their open confession of His name is like a crown upon two lives which have been lived as one in Christ. They have gone both of them together to a higher place in the affairs of this present life than they ever asked or thought. A reward even richer awaits them in the coming kingdom of the Lord Jesus Christ whom they served so faithfully here.

FIRST WORLD WAR

A period of military service in Ireland followed the years spent in Bermuda. It was while Dobbie was in Ireland that the Lord worked in such a way as to bring him to the place where his name was to come prominently before the world. Many years had come and gone since he passed through the Royal Military Academy as Woolwich. The fact that he had graduated among the first dozen men in his class might have seemed of little significance, during the period when he was laboring in an obscure corner of the world, but God had a purpose in it.

It was the custom to appoint two Royal Engineering officers to the Staff College at Camberley each year, together with some from various other branches of the service. They were chosen by competitive examination. Dobbie took the test in Ireland in the year 1911. He performed the brilliant feat of making the highest record of all the officers taking the examination. Entering the Staff College at once, he completed his training in 1913, while the world was preparing for the first great war.

When the young officer departed for France in August, 1914, he left behind him a family in which the oldest child, Arthur, was only eight. The younger boy was a baby of eighteen months. Ahead lay four years in which honors were to come to Dobbie, but much of suffering and danger as well.

Hardly had he arrived at the scene of battle, when his wife received a letter from him conveying the exciting news, "A most extraordinary thing has happened. They have given me the Legion of Honor." When the story came out later, it was learned that he had been assigned the responsibility for directing the traffic of the British troops during the terrible retreat from Mons. Many divisions had to be evacuated. Eight hours were required for one division with its equipment, to pass down the road. In consequence, someone had to be on duty twenty-four hours each day. Seven days were required for the retreat.

There was no opportunity for sharing the burden, nor did Dobbie ask for any. For an entire week he hardly left his horse. Finding that it was impossible to snatch a few winks of sleep on horseback without falling, he dismounted, stood with his head bowed over the top of a fence at the side of the road, and said to his orderly, "Wake me up in ten minutes." Then he resumed his arduous task of bringing order out of the confusion which threatened the surging mass of men and machines and all the paraphernalia making up an army on the move. One man said,

"That big man on the big horse! I shall never forget him. He was everywhere, and he never seemed to stop for rest."

After the troops had been successfully withdrawn, Dobbie was made a Chevalier of the Legion of Honor. The French government granted only two such awards for the entire division of nearly 20,000 men involved in the action at Mons. They were conferred upon the two outstanding officers.

Sir William experienced a number of narrow escapes. His wife saw in each of them an attempt by Satan upon the life of her husband because he sought to maintain a faithful testimony for Christ. On several occasions, when his life was in danger she was conscious of the personal animosity of the enemy of their souls.

The first incident of the kind came to Dobbie on the fields of France that same year. A hand grenade fell near him. When it exploded, a fragment struck him in the thigh. He was taken to a hospital tent. The surgeon remarked after an examination: "This is one of the nearest escapes from certain death that I have ever seen. The grenade fragment did not miss the main artery by more than the thickness of a piece of paper."

Because the piece of steel was found to be in such a position that it might have been fatal to attempt its removal, it was allowed to remain where it was. Sir William still carried it in his body when he came to America in 1945.

After spending his first Christmas of the first great war on a hospital train, Dobbie reached a hospital where he was placed in a bed just vacated by Captain (later General Sir) Arthur Smith, another Christian officer who had experienced a miraculous deliverance. The nurse remarked that it was most unusual to have two officers under her care in succession, who read their Bibles so constantly. When Dobbie inquired about the nature of the wound which had brought his friend to the hospital, he learned of one of the strangest miracles of the entire war.

Captain Arthur Smith's father had given him a pocket Bible to carry into battle. Inscribed on the flyleaf was a quotation from Psalm 91:9-11,

"Because thou hast made the Lord, which is my refuge,
    even the Most High, thy habitation;
"There shall no evil befall thee, neither shall any plague
    come nigh thy dwelling.
"He shall give His angels charge over thee, to keep thee
    in all thy ways."

A shell landed near the officer one night. The force of the explosion blew him across the road. When he recovered consciousness in the hospital, and was able to read, his father's Bible was given to him. It had been taken from the pocket of his tattered uniform, where it stopped a shell fragment and possibly saved his life.

The wonderful thing was the manner in which the frag-

ment had penetrated half way through the Bible, finding its
way out of the side between two of the leaves. When Captain
Smith carefully separated the pages, he found every one cut
and torn until he reached the middle. To his great astonish-
ment, the first page which had not been cut through by the
shell was the page from which the Scripture verses on the
flyleaf had been taken. The Bible verses his father had prayer-
fully chosen for him leaped up at him from the torn Book.
God had indeed given His angels charge over him. Thus,
these Christian officers of Britain's army witnessed the power
of their Saviour to keep them amid the dangers of battle.

Other honors came to Dobbie in that war. He received the
Distinguished Service Order (D.S.O.). Mention was made
of him seven times in dispatches. The French Legion of
Honor was followed by the Belgian Order of Leopold. The
greatest honor of all, however, came from the Throne of the
Universe. God heard his prayers from the battle field and sent
help from heaven when he needed it most.

While Dobbie was on Sir Douglas Haig's staff, in charge
of the disposition of troops on the western front, it became
necessary to move a division down from the north to meet
a heavy German attack. He called one of the railroad officials on the telephone.

"I want you to arrange for trains to pick up troops at stations in the north and move them down here."

"I am sorry; what you ask is impossible. We have no rolling stock on hand," replied the railway executive.

"You do not understand. Things are really touch and
go down here. We must have that division, and we must
have it at once."

"If we had the cars, we would place them at your disposal, but we are helpless. I repeat, there is no rolling stock
whatsoever."

When Dobbie hung up the telephone receiver, he knew

Air raid seen across Malta's farms.

Grand Harbor, Valetta.

A flower stall amid the ruins.

Anti-aircraft battery in action.

there was only one thing to do. A German break through might possibly have meant the loss of the war, at that critical time. In his extremity, he fell to his knees in the office, and prayed.

"Lord, I have come to the end of my tether. I do not know how we can bring that division down, but we must have those men. Please intervene."

In a few moments the telephone rang. It was the official to whom he had just been speaking.

"A most extraordinary thing has happened. There has come to hand a large amount of rolling stock, quite as much as we need. We cannot understand it; where it came from is a mystery, but we can have the trains ready at once."

The division was moved in, just in time to save the situation by plugging the line. The general in command was much impressed by the incident, as were all who learned of it, for it demonstrated that the help of God in answer to prayer was a tangible thing.

Only one other experience out of the ordeal of the first World War can find a place in these pages. It was during the darkness before the dawn of November 11, 1918. At five o'clock in the morning the telephone rang at British General Headquarters. It fell to the lot of Dobbie, as a member of the Operations Staff of Sir Douglas Haig, to answer the call. The representative of Marshal Foch, Generalissimo of the Allied armies, was on the wire announcing the signing of the Armistice.

Dobbie instantly dictated a telegram to all the troops of Britain on the western front,

"Hostilities will cease at 11:00 hours today. Troops will stand fast at the line reached at that hour. There will be no fraternization with the enemy."

In the strange providence which had brought this man of God to that place at that time, he had issued the order which stopped the first World War for Great Britain! It was twenty-five years, almost to the day, since peace had come to his own heart at his conversion. God's Word brought peace to him; his word brought peace to others. It was, in a sense, symbolic of his entire ministry as a servant of Christ.

SERVICE ABROAD

After the war was over, Dobbie served with the Army of Occupation in Germany. Because of his profound knowledge of the Bible, his fellow officers frequently sought him out to ask him about the teachings of the Scriptures. There had been much talk during the war about Armageddon. Speculation was rife that the end of the world was close at hand. Opportunity thus was given him for a real Bible teaching ministry during the comparatively quiet months he spent in Germany.

One of Britain's leading officers, who has since become very famous, made a practice of drawing Dobbie out in the presence of their superiors by saying, "Tell the General what you were telling me about the coming of the Lord." The two men made the most of such occasions. The results of such a witness to the high command are beyond calculation.

In 1919 Dobbie was awarded the title C.M.G., making him a Companion of the Order of St. Michael and St. George. In July of that year he was recalled to the War Office for staff appointments at home. He was made Brevet-Colonel in 1922, and Lieutenant Colonel in 1925. In this capacity he went to Egypt as Commander of the Royal Engineers.

After Dobbie was promoted to full Colonel in 1926, he was appointed General Staff officer, first grade, at the War Office from 1926 to 1928. He returned to Egypt in 1928 as Commander of the Cairo Brigade. In Cairo the Christian witness of his family took the form largely of ministry at the London Mission to the Jews. Lady Dobbie and Sybil taught in the mission school two or three times each week, where some twenty different nationalities were in attendance. Forty per cent of them were Jewish. As the children were converted they carried the gospel back to their homes.

It was during this period that Dobbie assumed command of the forces sent to Palestine in August, 1929, to suppress disturbances among the Arabs, and he was made a Major General.

A group of Christians determined to send a large number of Testaments to the troops in Palestine. They asked him to write an appropriate foreword to be included in each Testament. His statement revealed a personal interest in the souls of the men.

"You are stationed at the place where the central event in human history occurred, namely, the Crucifixion of the Son of God. You may see the place where this happened, and you may read the details in this Book. As you do this, you cannot help being interested, but your interest will change into something far deeper, when you realize that the event concerns you personally, and that it was for your sake that the Son of God died on the cross here. The realization of this fact cannot but produce a radical change in your outlook and in your life, and the study of this Book, will, under God's guidance, help you to such a realization."

Dobbie's office in Palestine was in the Government building just outside the Damascus Gate of the city of Jerusalem. From his desk he could look straight across to the hill of Calvary in front of him. From the window at his left was visible the garden in which it is believed the tomb of Christ was located.

Thus once more this servant of God found himself in a place where other famous Christians had preceded him, and he was once again to face a situation calling for implicit faith in Christ. In that office at Jerusalem he witnessed another of

those incidents so frequent in his experience, where heaven
was moved by the prayers of earth.

In the early days of his command in Palestine, before suf-
ficient troops had arrived to get the disturbances well in hand,
reports reached Dobbie's desk that a large body of armed
Bedouins was descending upon the city of Gaza from the
southeast. With no soldiers nearby for protection, the many
British women and children at the hospital in Gaza were in
serious danger from the wild men of the desert, said to number five thousand

Aircraft were sent to scare the band away by dropping
bombs in its path, but the Arabs were so well concealed in
the gullies and vegetation of the region that they were not
located from the air. Nothing more could be done for the
city. It lay helpless in the path of the oncoming horde.

Dobbie turned in this extremity to his Lord, as he had
in France during the other emergency years before. He
knelt there in his office, telling the Lord that he had done
what little he could for Gaza, but that divine intervention
was necessary. He specifically requested that God would
deliver the city from its enemies.

For a little while the reports indicated that the force was
still approaching. Then, suddenly, for no reason which
could be discovered, the Bedouins turned off at right angles
and the danger was past.

"I know God intervened," said Dobbie, "because prayer
was offered in the Name of His Son, the Lord Jesus Christ, a
Name which God always must honor."

Some years afterward, he met Dr. Hargreaves, who was
head of the hospital at Gaza in 1929. The doctor had been
absent on business in Jerusalem at the time of the incident.
The alarming reports had sent him likewise to his knees in
prayer for God's protecting hand over the nurses, and the
families of staff members at the hospital, including his own

wife and family. As the two men of God compared notes, they realized that they had been petitioning the throne of grace together. "If two of you shall agree on earth as touching anything that they shall ask, it shall be done for them of my Father which is in heaven."

Between the years of 1933 and 1935, Dobbie was Commandant of the School of Military Engineering and Inspector of Royal Engineers, after which he was appointed General Officer commanding Malaya. This gave him the opportunity for extensive travel in the far East. He made it a practice to look up the missionaries of the Brethren and the various denominations represented there, to encourage them in their service for Christ. Young Christian officers were invited to his home for Bible reading and prayers each Sunday evening, a custom of many years standing.

From Singapore Dobbie's testimony was sent out to the British army around the world. He had been invited to address a conference of Protestant chaplains. In the course of his remarks, he spoke in his usual straightforward and personal way to them:

"I order the men to march to church each Sunday. (Church attendance is compulsory in the British army.) I must therefore insist that they get something worth having when they attend. The soldiers want the real thing. They want you, their chaplains, to tell them what Jesus Christ means to you. They want to know about the help He has brought to you in your own experience.

"When you speak in this way, straight from the shoulder, about Christ as your own Saviour and Lord, then you will be giving the men what they need and what they are all seeking for. Only then will you be pulling your own weight in the Army."

Here was a member of the Plymouth Brethren, speaking in no uncertain terms to an assembly of ordained clergymen of the Established Church of England. To their everlasting credit be it said that the words of their commanding officer met with such an answering response in their hearts that they sent his message to their Journal. It was published and sent to every army station throughout the whole British Empire.

The rules of the British Army made it necessary for Dobbie to retire from active service at the age of 60, which he did on returning to England in August, 1919. Again it was in God's program for him that something which was a keen disappointment at the time, providentially became the circumstance out of which he was to find a new kind of service for the king of England and the King of kings.

World War II broke out with Dobbie chafing at his forced retirement. He immediately offered his services to the War Office in any capacity in which he might be of use. He was approached about two or three appointments, but they mysteriously failed to materialize. God had something better awaiting this man who had honored Him with his life. In April, 1940, the Chief of the Imperial General Staff asked him to take the post of Governor of the island of Malta.

With his instant acceptance, the most notable and far reaching experience in all of Dobbie's amazing career was to begin. The successful discharge of his duties as Governor was to have an effect upon Great Britain and America which no one could have anticipated

For Britain, the effect could be said to be predominantly temporal, in the disaster which was averted by his faith. For America, without detracting from the value to American arms of General Dobbie's work, one might say that the effect of his years on Malta was more largely spiritual. It was Malta which brought him before the American public more prominently than any other British General in generations. Had it not been for the miracle of Malta under Dobbie, thousands of American people might never have heard the gospel of the Lord Jesus Christ in one of the most unique ministries on record.

MALTA'S IMPORTANCE

The island of Malta has always occupied a place of tremendous importance in the central Mediterranean. A glance at the map makes it apparent why this should be, for it dominates the whole middle area of that sea. With the advent of the submarine and the airplane, its position became commanding.

Its enemies knew well that Malta would have to be reckoned a serious menace in time of war. The island was referred to as "that unsinkable aircraft carrier anchored off the heel of the Italian peninsula." Another familiar designation was, "that dagger ever pointing at the heart of Italy."

A German broadcast recorded shortly after Nazi bombs began to fall upon the tiny country declared, "Malta's importance can be understood if it is realized that it controls the most important trade routes to the Levant and to India. It controls the way from Gibraltar to the Suez Canal. History shows that the island has always been regarded as a key point in the Mediterranean. Napoleon prophetically foresaw the importance of the island." Reference to the life of Napoleon reveals what he said about the military value of the place, "Malta is the key that commands Europe."

The long history of the little country bears out everything which modern strategists have taught concerning its remarkable position. In the year 1530, when an advance into the Mediterranean by the Turks seemed inevitable, Emperor Charles V gave Malta to an order of the Crusaders called The Knights of St. John of Jerusalem.

Following thirty-five years of fortification by the Knights, the Turks attacked in 1565. For five months the island withstood a bloody siege. At length the Turks retired. Historians look upon the successful defence of Malta under Grand Master Jean de La Valette as one of the important battles of history, by which Europe was saved from Mohammedanism. If Malta was the bulwark of Christendom then, it was no less an invincible fortress holding back the tide of barbarism from 1940 to 1942.

Never had the tiny island been in a more hopeless case than when Dobbie arrived on April 28, 1940. The nearest British bases were Gibraltar, 900 miles to the west, and Alexandria, 900 miles to the east. Enemy territory was less than 60 miles away in Sicily. The seas were dominated by Italian and German aircraft on every side. It was the most isolated, helpless outpost of the empire imaginable. More than a quarter of a million people were crowded within its 92 square miles, in addition to the garrison of British soldiers, making it the most densely populated country in the world. All of its fuel and ammunition, and practically all of its food, had to be brought in over nearly a thousand miles of enemy seas where submarines lurked, beneath skies where hundreds of Axis planes kept watch to bomb every vessel in sight.

In spite of difficulties which seemed insurmountable, it was recognized that the fortress must be held at all costs. Looking backward upon the situation now, it is much easier to see the reasons why this was so than it was in the days when some British leaders considered that the island could not be defended successfully.

Italy maintained a large army in North Africa, but it had to be supplied across waters controlled by Malta. Later on, when Rommel had taken the field against Egypt, the same supply problem confronted him. Britain possessed a base for offensive action against every vessel seeking to transport Italian and German materiel, food, and reinforcements. It is very doubtful whether Rommel could have been successfully resisted, had more of the help reached him which started out from Italian ports. On several occasions every ship in southbound convoys headed for North Africa was sent to the bottom. Submarines operating from the island sank more than half a million tons of enemy shipping, in addition to what the airforce destroyed.

An official account of the work of the Royal Air Force in that theater was published by the British government, after the siege was lifted. It declared, "But for Malta, Rommel in 1942 might well have pressed on to Alexandria." Such a catastrophe would have prolonged the war indefinitely. It might even have meant final victory for the Axis.

The ports of the island rendered invaluable service. Not only could an underseas fleet be based there, but surface vessels as well. Cruisers and destroyers and lighter craft from Malta constituted an effective striking force. Several indispensable warships were saved from destruction by putting in at Valetta for repairs.

From the airfields of Malta reconnaisance pilots were able to keep the British fleet informed of enemy movements. Data supplied by them made possible the destruction wrought at Taranto, when a number of heavy units of the Italian navy were sunk or damaged. The victory of the Battle of Matapan could likewise be attributed in part to the work of pilots based on Malta.

The Commanding Air Officer received a message of appreciation from Commander-in-Chief Admiral Sir Andrew Cunningham, of the Mediterranean fleet, "Thank you for the most valuable reconnaissance work carried out by your squadrons, without which the successful attack on Taranto would have been impossible."

These same airfields enabled British and American pilots to range over the entire Mediterranean theater of war. Enemy movements were scrutinized on land and sea. Bombers being routed through the area were able to refuel on Malta. Even

Britain itself and the eastern battle front in Europe were benefited, because large numbers of German aircraft were diverted to Sicily and southern Italy, in an effort to bomb the island out of the war. This action was found necessary because of the terrible destruction Malta-based ships and planes wrought upon the enemy. In the month of November, 1941, more than a million bombs had been dropped on Axis targets.

When the German bombers came over, so many were shot down that the island came to be known as a bottomless drain down which the Luftwaffe poured its men and machines. Official figures listed 1129 enemy planes destroyed by the guns and aircraft defending the fortress. A larger number of German and Italian pilots were shot down than the total number of civilians killed during two years of intensive bombing.

DOBBIE ON MALTA

When Dobbie, walking in the footsteps of the Apostle Paul, stepped ashore on Malta, there were elements in the situation which must have reminded him of that salvation through Christ which had occupied so large a place in his thinking ever since he was a boy. There is to be found here an illustration of the gospel so faithfully proclaimed by the central character in this drama.

Malta was faced with the certainty of destruction, unless God should intervene on its behalf. It was weak; it was lonely; it was powerless to save itself. Strong and cruel enemies surrounded it on every side, intent upon its ruin. Fortunately, the island was aware of its desperate plight. Its attention was drawn to the fact that its only hope lay in help from above. It laid hold on that hope and cried to God for deliverance. Salvation from the Lord was forthcoming. Just as the destiny of mankind is linked to the eternal kingdom of God, so the destiny of the perishing island was inseparably connected with the earthly kingdom of Britain.

The new Governor arrived on Malta at a very critical time in the affairs of the British Empire. The summer of 1940 brought France into defeat. Dunquerque deprived England of most of her equipment. She stood alone before Germany, in much the same plight as her island fortress in the central Mediterranean. Dobbie could hope for no reinforcements from England for a long time to come. In point of fact, it was four months before any appreciable assistance was received. Every factor in the complicated problem facing the General had hopelessness written large upon it. Circumstances were such as to cause him to turn at once to God for help. Nevertheless, there can be no doubt that all of this was providential. God was working out an eternal purpose.

There were no aircraft on Malta to ward off bombing attacks until someone found four old Gladiators crated in the dockyards. They had been consigned to H.M.S. *Glorious,* but were overlooked when that aircraft carrier was last in port. Permission was secured to use them, although they were out of date. When they were assembled they were found to be too slow to catch the modern bombers of the Italian air force. A special technique was finally worked out by which they were able to achieve success in shooting down the enemy.

Sixteen obsolescent anti-aircraft guns were available for the defense of the entire island. The garrison numbered scarcely 5,000 men, a figure seen in its proper perspective when it is remembered that after the smaller island of Pantelleria was captured from the Italians, between 15,000 and 20,000 troops were found garrisoning it. For every square mile of territory on Malta, 2,700 civilians had to be fed, clothed, and protected. Thirty miles of invasion beaches needed to be patrolled. Plans for the defense had to take into consideration the possibility that every field on the interior might become a battleground, if an air invasion were attempted such as that which seized Crete.

The Italians had carried on an insidious propaganda for years, designed to undermine Britain's position and to win the allegiance of the Maltese for Italy. Fifth columnists were numerous; it was found necessary to deport a number of them at once. Tact and understanding would be required for the relations between Church and State, since the population was Roman Catholic and Dobbie was an ardent Protestant who represented almost the opposite pole of religious thinking. Malta's prospect's seemed anything but bright. The absence of any likelihood of reinforcement through Axis dominated seas completed the forbidding picture.

The Governor and his wife arrived early Sunday morning, April 28, 1940. Italy's declaration of war against Great Britain became effective at midnight, June 10th. Bombs began to fall on Malta the next day, June 11th, and they continued for over two years. There were eight air raids that first day. When the British government compiled figures on the subject and published them in the end of 1944, it was revealed that 2,315 air raids had killed 1,569 civilians; 24,000 buildings were destroyed or damaged by 14,000 tons of bombs. During that time the fortress became known all over the world as "the most bombed spot on earth." While the people huddled in caverns carved deep in the limestone rock, their houses and churches and lovely ancient buildings were blown into rubble over their heads. To read such a record of life on the island as Sybil Dobbie's *Grace Under Malta* is to be gripped by the heroism of a people who suffered the loss of everything they had, without flinching.

After word of Italy's declaration of war arrived, the hour of midnight between June 10 and June 11 was awaited with suspense. From the ramparts of Malta, Sir William and his little garrison of soldiers watched the skies and the sea for the invasion which was expected hourly. It never came.

"I have often thought about it, wondering why our enemies did not land under cover of darkness on that night or afterward," said the General. "I have been able to find only one reason for it. God in His mercy put out His restraining hand and kept them from attempting the invasion when they were able to do it. I can think of no other explanation for the strange blunder they seem to have made." There was not even an attack by the Italian navy, except for an abortive raid one year later by small torpedo boats, every one of which was destroyed by the watchful shore gunners.

One of the new Governor's first acts, after war had been declared, was to issue a special Order of the Day. He often quoted it to his audiences in America later, always with impressive results:

"The decision of His Majesty's Government to fight on until our enemies are defeated will have been heard with the greatest satisfaction by all ranks of the garrison of Malta. It may be that hard times lie ahead of us, but however hard they may be, I know that the courage and determination of all ranks will not falter, and that with God's help we will maintain the security of this fortress. I therefore call upon all officers and other ranks humbly to seek God's help, and then, in reliance upon Him, to do their duty unflinchingly."

Nothing could have had a deeper effect upon the soldiers as well as the civilians on Malta. This public declaration of dependence upon God won for their leader the enthusiastic loyalty of the Maltese, known for their religious fervor. His assurance that God would not suffer them to go down into defeat elicited such confidence in the men of the various services that they performed miracles of heroism in defending their posts and lashing out at the enemy. One officer said,

"I'll never be the skeptic I was before I served with Dobbie on Malta. He gave me something."

Said another, "He possesses an inner calm which is hard to explain."

This special Order of the Day reveals that the Governor knew beforehand how prayer would be answered and the fortress preserved. God gave him what his faith claimed. He acted upon what is written in Mark 11:23,

> "For verily I say unto you, That whosoever shall say unto this mountain, Be thou removed, and be thou cast into the sea; and shall not doubt in his heart; but shall believe that those things which he saith shall come to pass; he shall have whatsoever he saith."

Because he believed, he was given victory over great odds. The mountain of German and Italian aerial strength arrayed against Malta was literally cast into the sea in the sight of the island.

It is not difficult to find in the issuance of this Order an illustration of the manner in which Sir William's early life had been providentially guided by the Lord into channels calculated to prepare him for his greatest work. Back in the Royal Military Academy at Woolwich, he had read of Hezekiah. From the leader of Israel had come the example now followed, for Hezekiah had also faced superior forces encamped against his fortress cities, seeking to win them away from him. He had spoken comfortably to the people who looked to him for leadership,

> "Be strong and courageous, be not afraid nor dismayed for the king of Assyria, nor for all the multitude that is with him: for there be more with us than with him. With him is an arm of flesh; but with us is the Lord our God to help us, and to fight our battles" (II Chron. 32:7, 8).

Hezekiah's people had responded to their leader's appeal.

Dobbie's people on Malta did likewise. In both cases, God responded by granting miraculous deliverance.

THE HAND OF GOD

Within the greater miracle of the magnificent defence of Malta, there are a number of lesser miracles which delight the heart of the believer, like individual gems in a beautiful diadem. No account of the whole story of the island, nor of the several miracles God wrought there, can compare with General Dobbie's own book, *A Very Present Help.* He has written the record with matchless simplicity, completeness, and skill. He has given to the world a powerful and lasting testimony to the faithfulness of God. It is no part of our purpose to duplicate Sir William's work. A few brief incidents from the stirring days of the siege will suffice to convey a clear picture of what God wrought through His servant and those who stood with him.

The most famous of several notable answers to prayer to come out of the experiences of Malta under its praying leader has to do with the adventures of the aircraft carrier *Illustrious.* The ship was part of a naval force which had dared to defy the authority which the Axis boasted it then exercised over the entire Mediterranean.

German dive bombers concentrated their attack upon her when they found her escorting a convoy to the island from Gibraltar. So many hits were scored upon the carrier that she was obliged to enter the harbor of Valetta that night for emergency repairs.

The next morning the Germans came over in force to finish her off. Further severe damage was done by their bombs. Scant hope was held that the vessel could be made seaworthy, under the circumstances. The Luftwaffe rightly regarded her as a prize too valuable to lose, so they stepped up the fury of their attack.

The Governor was watching the situation with grave concern. He inquired how long it would take to complete the temporary repairs if the bombings should cease. "Four days, if we get no more damage," was the reply from the dockyard authorities. Prayer was offered to this end. The very next day, the German planes changed their tactics. They began to attempt high level bombing, but their aim was so poor that during the ensuing four days the ship was never struck! The *Illustrious* steamed away for Alexandria on the fourth evening, during a broadcast by the Italian radio which claimed she had been sunk and was lying on the bottom of the harbor of Valetta. She reached port in safety, to remain in the fighting until Italy and Germany were defeated.

On another occasion one of the cruisers based on Malta, H.M.S. *Penelope,* had to enter the drydock in the Grand Harbor for repairs. There the enemy planes found her, like a sitting duck, helpless to avoid their bombs. So often was she struck during these heavy raids that the crew rechristened her H.M.S. *Pepper Pot.* The strange thing was that no vital damage was done, either to the cruiser or to the dock in which she lay. The necessary repairs were at last completed. Looking very much like a porcupine because of the large number of wooden plugs sticking out everywhere, she left Malta and fought her way through to Gibraltar. On her arrival the crew was called on deck for a service of thanksgiving and praise for deliverance from the continuous attacks during the voyage. Prayer had wrought another miracle.

General Dobbie maintained his offices as Governor in the palace of Valetta. It was his custom to go home for lunch at the same hour each day. On one occasion Lady Dobbie was surprised to see him returning to their palace at San Anton some forty minutes earlier than usual. When she asked him the reason, he had no explanation to offer. With no preconceived purpose of changing the schedule, he had suddenly

German bombs bursting on Valetta.

Unloading a convoy by night.

Searchlights and anti-aircraft fire during a night attack.

Cathedral illuminated by enemy flares.

decided to dismiss his staff and return home nearly an hour before the accustomed time.

Hardly had he arrived at San Anton, when Lady Dobbie received a telephone call from Valetta. Soon after the offices had been vacated, a heavy bomb had fallen near that part of the palace. The Governor's offices and the adjoining rooms used by other governmental officials were wrecked and rendered uninhabitable.

This was another example of the protecting power of God as He kept watch over His own. Such occurrences were so frequent in the lives of the Governor and his helpers that a phrase came to be used in the household to describe these events, "Seeming accident but invisible guidance."

The impression made upon his associates and upon the people of the island by Sir William's faith was astonishing. The Maltese, so intensely religious that they spoke of themselves as "more Catholic than the pope," recognized the living reality of their leader's trust in God. They heard him broadcasting to them over the radio, saying, "Over and above our toil we need the help and deliverance of Almighty God." They listened as he exhorted them to trust in the Lord and to show their faith by hard work in the defense of their land.

They saw the Governor with their Archbishop ministering to their needs after every serious air raid. They knew he regularly visited all the Protestant Parade Services, worshipping at each of them by turns on Sundays. They came to believe that he bore a charmed life. The facts confirmed this, for he was never hit by the enemy. San Anton palace, his home on Malta a few miles outside Valetta, was like an island in the midst of widespread destruction. Bombs fell all about it; some glass was broken in its windows, but the Palace itself was never struck.

A British Press Service dispatch from Malta said of the General, "Foremost among the soldiers and citizens of this beleaguered little island is a 'large man with a great heart,' who pitches in to help his air raid wardens extricate wounded men and women from the wreckage of their homes, and then returns to inspire his men in the battle against almost overwhelming odds from the air. . . .

"In the words of one of his officers, Dobbie will 'go out in the hottest Luftwaffe attacks, imperturbable, regardless of himself, thoughtful only for others.' A militant Protestant, he is chairman of the Officers' Christian Union and a recognized authority on the Bible. In one of several pocket sized books on the Bible that he has written for Army use, 'Christianity and Military Service,' Dobbie reveals his own convictions.

" 'It will thus be seen,' he concludes, 'that the Scripture indicates that the profession of arms is an honorable and lawful one: that the use of force and material weapons is not incompatible with faith in God: that God is a God of order who has ordained that human government shall maintain order with force: that the time is not yet, though it will surely come, when the government will be on His shoulder, and man will be able to beat his sword into a ploughshare'."

A *Time* reporter cabled, "During the hottest raids, air raid wardens would find Sir William beside them, unruffled, pitching in to help move wounded out of bomb-wrecked houses."

One young British officer said of his commander, "Dobbie paid no more attention to bombs and machine gun fire than to rain. He was in the tower of the palace roof when the Germans, trying to get the crippled *Illustrious,* concentrated more fire power on Valetta at the dockyard than has ever been released on any other spot on earth."

Perhaps the finest testimony of all to the true Christian character of General Dobbie comes from the Roman Catholic

Archbishop of Malta. It is best expressed by Frances Gerard, a Roman Catholic writer, in his *Malta Magnificent:*

"The Archbishop-Bishop's pronouncement was unforgettable. I trust he will forgive my paraphrasing his exact words. 'All my life,' he said, ' I have read, in the Lives of the Saints and elsewhere, of that queer look which was observed to come over the faces of certain saints when speaking of God. It has been described as a mystic radiance, which seemed to light up their countenances from within. I, myself, have met it but once in a long lifetime. That was in the present Governor.' High praise, high praise indeed, from the Catholic Archbishop-Bishop of the British General, who was a Plymouth Brother —Dobbie of Malta."

Behind the outward evidences of His favor which God was pleased to give to His servant, there were the private devotions of which we are afforded a glimpse by some who were present. *Moody Monthly* carried in one issue the substance of a broadcast in London by Commander A. Kimmins which gives us a part of the picture.

The broadcast referred to General Dobbie as "a big man— big physically, big professionally, and big morally. He has the reputation of fighting with a sword in one hand and a Bible in the other." Said Commander Kimmins, "As one who has had the honor to be a guest of General Dobbie and Lady Dobbie during the present siege of Malta, I would like to mention how impressive General Dobbie can be. His charming house at San Anton is run with the dignity befitting a representative of the King, combined with the simplicity of a soldier. After dinner the guests proceed to the drawing room, where, standing in front of the fireplace, General Dobbie says, 'It is usual in this house to say a few words of thanks to Almighty God,' and then, for a minute or so, he offers a prayer of thanks for the day and its events."

It was early in the days of the attack that the custom was

begun of conducting devotions for the palace party and guests, after dinner. Sir William said to them one evening as he rose from the table,

"As head of the palace, Governor of the Island, and representative of the King, I want to acknowledge God in this house. It is proper that we should pray for our cause, for Malta, and for our own people. Any who may not care to pray with us must not think that we shall feel offended. 'As for me and my house, we will serve the Lord.'"

As they were ascending the eleven steps which connected the dining room with the adjoining library, Lady Dobbie wondered how many of their friends (some of whom were Catholics) would join them in prayers. At the top of the stair she turned. Every one of them was coming in for devotions. It was a custom followed every night thereafter. Frequently there were distinquished guests at the palace. Always they joined in the brief time of worship and prayer, unless they were obliged to leave for the airport. Lord Wavell and other guests stood with the Governor while he offered heartfelt prayers and expressed thanksgiving to God for His goodness.

In this, as well as in the regular Bible reading Sir William maintained for the officers, is to be seen the real secret of Malta's preservation and final victory. The hand of God was revealed in answer to the faith of a Christian leader and his people.

RECOGNITION AND REWARD

The fame of Malta rapidly spread over the world. Cablegrams and citations poured in from everywhere, to the surprise of its leaders and its citizens, who thought the island too obscure to merit such attention amid the flaming events of the great war.

The President of the United States sent word to Malta's defenders from America, on December 7, 1943:

"In the name of the people of the United States of America, I salute the Island of Malta, its people and defenders, who, in the cause of freedom and justice and decency throughout the world, have rendered valorous service far above and beyond the call of duty.

"Under repeated fire from the skies, Malta stood alone but unafraid in the center of the sea, one tiny bright flame in the darkness——a beacon of hope for the clearer days which have come.

"What was done in this Island maintains the highest traditions of gallant men and women who from the beginning of time have lived and died to preserve civilization for all mankind."

FRANKLIN D. ROOSEVELT

Americans were thrilled when Malta and Corregidor exchanged greetings. Referring to the Philippine fortress under siege by the Japs as "an American competitor for the honor of being the most blasted spot on earth," *Newsweek* reported, "To Lieut. Gen. Jonathan M. Wainwright at Corregidor on the other side of the earth, Dobbie expressed on behalf of the people of Malta 'profound admiration for the fortress' magnificent fight.' Wainwright replied that American troops in the Philippines had been 'inspired and encouraged by Malta's historic stand.' " Help did finally come to the Mediterranean garrison; none arrived at far away Corregidor.

The proudest reward given to the people of the island was received from the King, while Dobbie was still Governor. The Secretary of State for the Colonies relayed the message,

"I have it in command from the King to convey to you the following message: 'TO HONOUR HER BRAVE PEOPLE I AWARD THE GEORGE CROSS TO THE ISLAND FORTRESS OF MALTA TO BEAR

WITNESS TO A HEROISM AND DEVOTION
THAT WILL LONG BE FAMOUS IN HISTORY.
                    GEORGE R. I.

Sir William explained to the Maltese that the George
Cross is the highest prize ever given for civilian valor. What
the king had done was quite unique in the history of the
British Empire. It was the first and only time that an entire
community had been so signally honored.

After the American carrier *Wasp* had gone to the relief
of the island by taking in squadrons of Spitfires which turned the tide of the air warfare, and after other aid had been
received, one of the original four Gladiators was presented
to the people of Malta as a memorial of the early days of the
battle.

It was a testimony to the biblical character of the leadership of Malta, that the three Gladiators which bore the brunt
of the fighting after one of the famous aircraft was destroyed, were called *Faith, Hope,* and *Charity.* A striking statement about this is to be found in the official British publica-
tion, *The Air Battle of Malta,* the record of the work of the
Royal Air Force during the period from June, 1940 to November, 1942.

"In presenting *Faith,* now sole survivor, to the people of
Malta on the third of September, 1943, Air Vice-Marshal Sir
Keith Park said that during the first five months of the
war these three Gladiators, with a handful of Hurricanes,
intercepted 72 enemy formations and destroyed or damaged
37 enemy machines. 'The defense of Malta,' he added, 'can
justifiably be included among the epics of this war, and
Faith has earned a place of honour in the armour of Malta."

How truly Sir Keith Park spoke! The battered but victorious airplane was but the symbol of the faith of a great leader
and a pious people who looked to God for their defense. Here
indeed is a case where Faith — faith in God — earned a place

of honor in the armor which protected the island fortress from its foes.

It is noteworthy that while there is but one reference to Sir William in this entire booklet of 96 pages about the air battle of Malta, that one reference contains a mention of his trust in the Lord.

"The Governor's broadcast to the people included these words: 'The safety and well being of this fortress rests *under God* on four supports. They are the three fighting services and the civil population. Each one of these is essential to the well being of the others, and each one depends on the other three and cannot do without them.' "

After two years as Governor, Sir William relinquished his post on Malta. It was in May of 1942, and the air raid sirens were sounding for the 2300th time, as he awaited the plane which was to carry him away. With keen regret that he could not have remained until the shadow of the Luftwaffe was gone entirely from the place he had defended so valiantly for so long, the General quietly left the palace with his family and was driven to the air field. Reasons of military security forbade their taking leave even of old friends and servants.

Lord Gort, Dobbie's successor, had come in on the plane which was to take him out. The two men held a consultation while the flying boat was being refueled, and while the sirens sounded a raid and bombs began to fall on the island. Then Sir William joined his wife and daughter, the plane took off in the darkness, and Dobbie of Malta was gone.

As the company neared Gibraltar at the end of the first leg of the journey to England, they were permitted a heartening sight, a token of the bright future awaiting Malta after the last hours of the night of her trial. They looked down upon the waters of the Mediterranean and saw a large convoy headed for the island. Among the supplies it carried were a number of Spitfires, which took to the air as soon as they were unloaded and prepared for action. An attacking fleet of German planes was dispersed with losses so great that the Luftwaffe never again returned in such force. It was the beginning of the end of the siege. God had given Dobbie the privilege of seeing the promise of this victory, even before the plane which carried him from Malta had reached its destination.

At London a large crowd waited at the airport to welcome him. There were audiences with the King, the Prime Minister, and other leaders of the Empire. The London *Times* published a full length portrait of the Dobbie family group, with a glowing account of the official celebration of the return of the successful defender of Britain's island outpost. King George VI honored the General by making him a Knight Grand Cross of St. Michael and St. George (G.C.M.G.).

Sir William arrived on May 10th. Even before the necessary functions were over, he was seriously ill. By May 15th, his temperature had reached 105 degrees. After being taken to the military hospital at Aldershot, Dobbie was found to have a ruptured appendix, and an operation was performed immediately.

Complications made a second operation necessary. His heart occasioned grave alarm. An experienced nurse said his pulse was faster than anything she had ever known in all her service. Lady Dobbie and their son were with him every hour during the crisis. She felt then, as she had on several previous occasions, the enmity of the adversary being directed against her husband. But Sir William rallied. After six weeks he was taken from the hospital to the Isle of Wight for another six weeks of convalescence. Churchill, who referred to the General as "that determined and resolute leader," sent flowers during this critical time, and the royal palace frequently telephoned to inquire about him.

Prayer, born of real faith in God, had preceded Dobbie's achievement on Malta. Prayer was his vital breath during his Governorship. Characteristically, one of the first items of news about him after his arrival in Britain told of his attending a prayer meeting with his son. Under the headline, DOBBIE OF MALTA PRAYS IN ENGLAND, the London *Daily Express* published the story.

"Within a few hours of reaching home yesterday, Dobbie of Malta want to a private prayer meeting near his son's house at Camberley, Surrey . . . At a Home Counties airport to meet him was his son, Lieut. Colonel Arthur Dobbie. And last night father and son went to the prayer meeting, which was held in the drawing room of Crawley Ridge, the home at Camberley of Captain Godfrey Buxton, a personal friend of General Dobbie.

"During the service General Dobbie offered a prayer for the safety of Malta and for its continued resistance. Fewer than twenty people were at the meeting and none of them knew before the service that General Dobbie was in England.

"'We were surprised when he walked in,' Captain Buxton said after the service, 'but it is typical of the man that, tired as he is after his journey from Malta and worn out with the strain of meeting so many people on this his first day back in England, he should still find time to come and give thanks to God.' "

During the General's convalescence, Lady Dobbie asked Sir William what he should like most to do after his retirement, which took place in November of the same year. His reply was, "The thing I should like to do most of all would be to witness to the saving grace of the Lord Jesus Christ everywhere." God gave to His servant just what his heart desired. Forty nine years had passed since the new birth had

brought rest to his own soul. His government gave him rest
from his arduous duties, almost on the anniversary of his
conversion. The two experiences together brought him to
an altogether unexpected public ministry for the Lord he
loved.

Sir William was invited all over England to address large
audiences. A member of the family who knew the details of
this itinerant ministry, marked upon a map with red ink each
place where his testimony was given. After two years had
been devoted to the work, the map was nearly covered with
red marks. Uncounted thousands heard his powerful witness
for Christ. Salvation had come to Malta under his Governorship; salvation came to many of the people of England because he was appointed to an Ambassadorship of the King
of Kings and Lord of Lords. There can be no doubt that
his last work was the greater. It was a fitting crown to a life
of faithful service for the Saviour whose cause he had espoused
half a century before.

II
THE MISSION

General Dobbie's American Tour

THE REASON FOR HIS COMING

THERE were very few people in the United States who saw clearly the thing of supreme importance which was happening at Malta during the tragic days of its siege. Why was God so wonderfully preserving that tiny isle from the massed might of the strongest military force in all history? Why was it that the resistance of a handful of soldiers, pilots and sailors on an isolated outpost of the British Empire could not be overcome by the millions of men at the disposal of the enemy, his thousands of warplanes, or his navy, which had boasted that it could bring about the overthrow of the fortress within two days?

We are well aware now, of course, of the strategic issues of the Battle of Malta. We do not overlook the military significance of the island. We acknowledge that had it fallen, Allied power in the Mediterranean would have received a blow from which it could not have recovered for years, if at all. The key to the successful defense of Egypt lay in the maintaining of an offensive base at Malta. Had the island been overwhelmed, and Egypt lost, it is easy to understand how Germany and Japan could have joined hands through the Suez Canal and prolonged the war for years.

From the viewpoint of eternity, however, there was something of far greater importance involved than this military situation, important as it admittedly was. Empires wax and wane. The tides of conquest advance and recede. Yet the eternal purpose of God moves on irresistibly. Nothing can thwart it. No one can delay it. No event can possibly defeat its smallest detail.

God has revealed that He is engaged in taking a company of people out of the world for Himself. The progress of the

gospel is of more moment than the destiny of an empire, in
His sight. The whole world is not to be compared in value
with one human soul. The nations are a drop in a bucket.
The material creation is the work of His fingers, but He has
bared the right arm of His power in bringing salvation to
men.

What was going on in the Mediterranean between 1940
and 1942 was linked with God's sovereign program for saving the lost, even though this was unsuspected by the world,
which was able to see only the great military events and the
romance of a brave people fighting and winning against
incredible odds.

Behind the scenes at Malta there was in course of preparation a new phase in the strategy of quite another war, carried
on ceaselessly between the forces of God and the forces of
Satan. The Lord was preparing the background for a ministry
of soul winning destined to reach uncounted numbers of the
British and American public previously almost untouched by
the message of the cross of Christ.

The world was giving front page headlines to the miracle
of Malta's resistance. General Dobbie was becoming a household name to millions. His unswerving faith in God was
being demonstrated under the most difficult circumstances.
Press and radio were uniting to declare that here was a man
of high culture and commanding position, a man who was
likely to be an international figure on the pages of history
books for generations to come. Yet, here was also a man who
was known to all as a humble, God fearing Christian who
made no secret of the fact he had taken the Lord Jesus Christ
as his Saviour.

In the providence of God, while the fortress of Malta was
trembling under the weight of the bombs being dropped
upon it, and its darkest hour had come, with the outcome
hanging in the balance, a vision of the eternal issues of the

uneven struggle was given in a land where General Dobbie had never set foot, the United States of America.

At the Moody Bible Institute of Chicago, the scene on Malta was being watched with unusual interest. It was realized that God might there be preparing an instrument for the evangelizing of a class of people who had not been effectively reached with the gospel for an entire generation.

In every large city in America there are missions for the "down and outers," where unfortunate men and women are provided with some of the necessities of life and given at the same time the remedy for their difficulties from the Word of God. There are churches in practically every community, ministering chiefly to the middle classes. Almost untouched, however, has been a large segment of the population consisting of respectable middle and upper class people who remain aloof from organized Christianity. They are sometimes referred to as the "up and outers." No missions have been established to reach them. They do not enter the churches where they might hear the gospel and be saved.

This was the group for whom it was hoped that God might be preparing a special messenger amid the stirring events taking place in the Mediterranean. The name and fame of Dobbie were well known to them. Doctors, lawyers, military and naval officers, professors, statesmen, business leaders — people of wealth and culture, of high moral and social standing, would be attracted to such a man as Lieutenant General Sir William George Sheddon Dobbie, G.C.M.G., K. C. B., D.S.O., LL.D., Colonel Commandant of Royal Engineers, Governor of Malta, hero and leader of men extraordinary. Thousands could be expected to come and hear him, who would not think of attending a conventional evangelistic meeting.

The same divine hand which had guided the General throughout his life and given him such a notable place in

contemporary history, was in evidence in the magnitude of
the plans made for him in the United States and Canada. The
Moody Bible Institute carried on correspondence with him
for nearly two years, with a view to arranging an American
tour after the completion of his ministry in Britain. When
at last it was possible for a definite date to be suggested,
and Dr. Will H. Houghton, President of the Institute, wrote
to Sir William urging him to come and tell America of his
Saviour and Lord, the answer came,

"I feel it a great privilege and an honour to be allowed
to speak for Christ and of Him."

The General's conviction that it was God's will for him
to accept the invitation meant that he would permit nothing
to stand in his way. Therefore he sacrificed a very great
honor which had been offered to him, in order that he might
preach Christ in the United States. Sir William was invited
to be the Representative Colonel Commandant of Royal Engineers for 1945, the expected year of victory, in accordance
with a British custom whereby one outstanding officer of the
Royal Engineers is designated each year to represent His
Majesty, the Colonel-in-Chief of the Corps, at important functions. He declined, counting his ambassadorship for Christ
a higher honor.

In the United States arrangements were made for the General to appear before Congressmen at Washington, and to
address the most exclusive clubs and the most conservative
university gatherings in leading cities and educational centers.
Mass meetings were planned in the largest auditoriums available in strategic locations where entire metropolitan areas
could have the opportunity of hearing him.

Chambers of Commerce gladly set aside plans of long
standing so that business men might be able to listen to Dobbie. Radio stations gave him time on the air when their lis-
tener audiences were largest. Newspapers featured his coming

Valetta street scene after a raid.

Valetta's opera house.

Ancient cavern used as communal shelter.

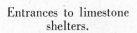

Entrances to limestone shelters.

as a notable event. Reporters were on hand to take down his words and give them large space in their next editions.

Lady Dobbie, an excellent speaker in her own right, was given an enthusiastic hearing by social leaders everywhere. Her university appearances brought her before thousands of assembled students. America received the famous visitors with open arms and receptive minds. And always, wherever either of them spoke, there was a definite, uncompromising presentation of the claims of the Saviour upon the hearts of those who heard.

AMERICAN IMPRESSIONS

It is an interesting fact that the arrival of Sir William and Lady Dobbie coincided with the diamond jubilee of another event which had a similar effect of binding Christians in America and Britain together. Just sixty years before the General arrived in Chicago for the Founders' Week Conference of the Moody Bible Institute —sixty years to the very day—the famous "Cambridge Seven" had set sail from Britain for China as missionaries under the China Inland Mission.

These were seven young men, best known of whom was C. T. Studd, who were led to give their lives to Christ as foreign missionaries as the direct result of D. L. Moody's evangelistic work at Cambridge in 1882. An American evangelist had brought about their decision. In turn, American universities had been stirred by their action to begin a Student Volunteer Movement. Britain and America were brought together as never before by the movement of the Spirit of God at that time.

On February 5, 1945, exactly sixty years after the culmination of those events, Lieutenant General Sir William Dobbie stepped from a train in the city of Chicago to conduct meetings as a British evangelist in Moody's city. Yet such was his unique position and ministry that no one thought of applying the term "evangelist" to him. The total effect of his preaching was to bring America and Great Britain closer together in the bonds of Christian love and understanding. No one can calculate how many young people in American Universities, as well as individuals from all walks of life, were inspired by his meetings to devote their energies to the service of Christ at home and abroad.

When the General appeared before the Founders' Week Conference, after having spoken several times in the East on his way to the Windy City, his audience numbered thousands of Christians who were accustomed to hearing the finest expositors of the Word in the English speaking world. As Sir William arose to address the gathering in the great Moody Church, very few knew what to expect from the typically British soldier who stood before them, tall and dignified, almost a legendary figure in the history of the second World War.

If any had come to hear exciting tales of military action, of terror by night and destruction by day, they were disappointed. Of necessity, the General had to recount some of the events on Malta which had given him such prominence before the American people. Every such incident he related, however, was with the object of glorifying his Saviour. From the first word he uttered, he had only one purpose in view, to persuade men and women to give the Lord Jesus Christ the pre-eminence in all things.

The audience sat enthralled by what was to them a new technique in public speaking. There was the sweetness of the humility of Christ to be seen in Sir William's demeanor, certainly. There were all the graces of a cultured Scot, a gentleman to his fingertips. There were the quiet assured tones of a man accustomed to command, yet now pleading on behalf of the One to whom he was glad to render implicit obedience.

There was the poise of one who had often stood in the presence of world leaders as one of their peers, but who now spoke as in the solemn and awful presence of his God.

The thing of which this select American audience took note was something different from all these. It was of the essence of the difference between British and American patterns of thought and expression. In a word, the General was seen to be master of understatement. This was what impressed men more than his English accent or the way he turned a phrase.

With entire unconsciousness of any seeking after dramatic effect, Sir William was nevertheless able to achieve something which Hollywood has sought vainly to attain by exaggeration and the multiplying of adjectives. He produced a deep, lasting effect upon his hearers by habitually refraining from all terms except the very mildest, as he spoke of events which seemed to demand stronger language by their great importance.

Referring to the dark days of the beginning of the siege, when he was sorrounded by powerful foes who presented him with a situation so apparently hopeless as to make many another leader despair of anything except a speedy and bitter defeat, the General might be expected to choose such words as would produce the maximum effect in portraying the gravity of what lay ahead for Malta. Instead, he simply said,

"We found ourselves confronted with problems of an unusual nature. The island was not a convenient place to defend."

Describing the pitiful lack of equipment when the war began, he was able to state the case as no American would,

"Our human resources were inadequate to make sure we could hold Malta."

About the shortage of men to defend the fortress, he said,

"It would have been nice if we could have had a strong

garrison on the island."

This characteristic puzzled and delighted reporters all over the country. They would tell their readers how this "huge, lumbering, typical professional soldier speaks nearly always in understatements." He was described as "neither pompous nor dogmatic, a man who expressed his beliefs with great simplicity."

Then they would forget themselves and relapse into typical American newspaper language. According to their accounts of the interviews they held, Sir William found the immense size of the country "staggering." He "marveled" because "you travel all day in America, and in the evening you look at a map and find you have gone only an inch or two." Lady Dobbie "gasped" at the shops which were "bulging with things England had not seen in years." In one city the discovery was even reported that the General considered the abundance of eggs "the most impressive thing" which had come under his observation in the United States.

When the newsmen noticed that Dobbie, like most Britishers, was a stranger to American slang, they slyly introduced as much of it as possible when they talked with him. He heard of skin games and kibitzers, of being beaten to the draw and getting the drop on an enemy. Not to be outdone, he gave the reporters a solemn quotation which they took down verbatim.

"If we of the Allied nations are going to win the peace as well as the war, we are going to have to pull up our own socks," he said in answer to a serious question.

"Translate that into English," they requested.

"Why, that's perfectly good English," he replied, "every Englishman would know exactly what I mean."

Not until he had completed the interview, and received an explanation for every American slang phrase used in his presence, did he tell the bewildered reporters that "pulling up one's own socks" is British for "keeping one's chin up."

Sir William and Lady Dobbie arrived at New York city on Friday, January 19, 1945. They were met at the pier by Dr. Houghton, President of the Moody Bible Institute. One of the first calls they made was at the City Hall, where they were introduced to Mayor LaGuardia, in the presence of the British Consul General. While Dobbie was talking with the Mayor, the air raid warning system was being given its regular weekly test. As the sirens sounded, he cocked his ears and smiled. "I feel quite at home," he remarked.

Traveling to Washington, D. C., by train, the visitors were surprised to see the "restaurant cars" in which they dined. "In England, even the King carries his lunch while traveling," they explained. The capital city frankly delighted its distinguished guests with its beauty. They regarded it as the most beautiful city they had ever seen. Especially they admired the view of the Capitol and its surrounding buildings as seen from Union Station. The weather, however, was "jolly cold."

The descriptions of the General appearing in papers all over the country were illuminating. One mid-western reporter compared him to "David with a slingshot outwitting Goliath," when Malta "held out through divine grace against the immeasurably superior power of the Axis." This recognition of the part God played in the success of the island's defense was clear evidence that the General did not fail to give the Lord the glory due His name, even in his interviews. Such news reports quietly but effectively enlarged Dobbie's testimony throughout the country.

The religious column of a newspaper in the South carried the comment, "With all his earthly titles, Lieutenant General Dobbie is just a humble Christian, fearlessly proclaiming his faith in the Lord Jesus Christ as his Saviour."

Said the leading editorial in an Eastern daily,

"Too many citizens have been stirred by the message brought to this city by Lt. Gen. Sir William and Lady Dobbie to have their influence end with their departure. These deeply religious, sturdily consecrated Christians go about on this Continent giving testimony to the help of God, not only in saving the island of Malta where they lived under siege but in all other circumstances of life.

"Not without precedent but still unusual is it for persons of their station in life on this as well as the other side of the ocean to spend their time on such missions. One can only hope that it may start a fashion in the United States and in this city for men and women who believe just as fervently as General and Lady Dobbie to tell their neighbors and others about a matter as vital to them as it is to this titled English pair."

Wrote a columnist in a famous newspaper in the Mississippi valley,

"I have just met a great man. I've met several great men in my span of years, but outside the clergy, it is seldom that one meets an individual, particularly a soldier, who is neither ashamed, embarrassed, nor afraid to express in public a deep, unshakable faith in God Almighty and love for His Son, Jesus Christ."

To read such comments from news writers who were accustomed to meeting hundreds of public figures and writing their stories, is to realize that God worked in a mighty way through Sir William and Lady Dobbie as they gave their witness to America.

AN UNUSUAL MINISTRY

It became evident early in the American tour that here was a messenger of the cross of Christ who could gain entrance to the most exclusive circles of society in this country. He bore his firm testimony in the most unusual places, where seldom had anyone ever sounded the note of salvation through the shed blood.

In Washington, a joint session of the House and Senate breakfast groups overstayed its customary hour while Dobbie spoke to them of Christ. In every city leaders in the business and professional worlds sat at luncheon and heard the General's address. Influential folks who would not attend a mass meeting or an evangelistic service, counted it an honor to be present while Sir William, with outspoken firmness but with such consummate grace and courtesy that no one could feel that he had taken advantage of them, spoke of the love of the Saviour in dying for sinners such as he.

Many universities in the United States and Canada thought it fitting to have their presidents introduce these distinguished guests as they appeared before student assemblies. Governor of states and mayors of great cities stood on the platform with the General and expressed pleasure at the opportunity for speaking a few words about the importance of his contribution to the conduct of the war by his defense of Malta.

Sir William and Lady Dobbie were luncheon guests of Mrs. Franklin D. Roosevelt in the White House at Washington. The President was out of the city at the time. The General left a copy of his book, *A Very Present Help*, for America's first family to read. The visit made such a deep impression on Mrs. Roosevelt that she spoke of the General on three different occasions in her syndicated newspaper column, a fact which did not escape other columnists.

After sitting up late to read Sir William's book, the First Lady quoted a paragraph from it in her next article. She selected his comparison between Malta in 1940 and Dothan in the days of Elisha.

"We were in the position of the servant who saw the enemy's hosts around the city: 'Alas, my master, how shall we do?' Elisha's answer means much to all who turn to God in their difficulties. 'Fear not, for they that be with us are more than they that be with them.' " Referring to Dobbie's book again on another day, Mrs. Roosevelt wrote two paragraphs on the need for prayer in America's national effort, such as was offered on the island of Malta under Sir William.

It was in Washington that Lady Dobbie gave her first address to be reported in the press. A selected audience had gathered to hear her speak in the chapel of the Central Union Mission of the Churches. According to the newspapers, it was "a red letter occasion, when nobility entered the doors of the Mission for the first time."

Her message was straightforward and true to the Word. Its theme was Jesus Christ the Rock. She linked the island of Malta to the Scriptures by describing the refuges which were carved out of the limestone of which the island is formed. When death threatened the people, they fled for refuge to the protection of the rock which had been provided for them. Christ is the Rock of Ages, cleft for sinners. All who flee to Him find shelter and perfect security. Some on Malta did not take advantage of the salvation prepared for them, and they perished. If any fail to take refuge in Christ, destruction is certain to overtake them. There was more than enough room in the caverns of the island; there is room for all in Christ. No one need perish. Whosoever will, may come to Him and be saved.

"Malta had a wonderful system of underground passages," she said, "we didn't know how extensive they were until this war. People have tried to seize the island many times in the past. The earliest inhabitants knew the value of the passages. The Maltese are Phoenicians, descendants of Hannibal. I was once in a temple they told me was 5,000 years old, dedicated to some awful heathen god. Everyone who did not go to the communal shelters would dig his own shelter in the backyard, and they were always breaking into some great subterranean room, dug out centuries before."

Lady Dobbie added another story to the many anecdotes of the wonderful way in which God answered their prayers while they were on Malta. Their daughter had been in Singapore at the time Sir William was made Governor of the island. He sent for her to come and help him as his private secretary.

Sybil started her long trip by airplane, but on arriving in Egypt she learned that it would be necessary to complete the journey by ship from Alexandria. The interesting record of the entire experience appears in her book, *Grace Under Malta*. With the utmost secrecy, a convoy was made up and started for the island. She was aboard one of the merchant vessels.

The trip was rather uneventful until submarines attacked them when they were well along their way. Depth charges were dropped by the escorting destroyers, with good success. As the convoy drew nearer to its destination, Sybil was somewhat disappointed when a heavy overcast obscured everything from view. She had been looking forward to her first sight of the island. The overcast continued until the ships anchored in Grand Harbor at Valetta.

In the meanwhile, Sir William and Lady Dobbie had received word that the convoy was nearing Malta. A heavy raid was in progress. It was known that planes were also searching for the ships from Alexandria. If they could be attacked in force, the chances were that most of the vessels would be sunk.

The General and his wife turned to the Lord in prayer and asked Him to save their child. Hardly had they finished praying when God answered by sending a thunderstorm. It was accompanied by such a widespread area of clouds and fog that the Luftwaffe was forced to return to its bases in

Sicily. Not one plane was able to interfere with the safe arrival of the entire convoy.

The American tour had not progressed very far before it was seen that Sir William's position was so unusual that he was able to overcome prejudice and attract a class of hearers usually untouched by Protestantism.

Something reminiscent of the high regard in which he was held by the Roman Catholic people of Malta occurred, when an American Roman Catholic weekly quoted a part of one of the General's addresses with evident approval. *The Sunday Visitor* has long been known for the outspoken way in which it attacks the Protestant Church. Yet it turned from its established policy to publish a statement by Dobbie.

Under the headline, "A Practical Thing," it quoted him,

"Being a Christian is a very practical thing. From the human side there is no explanation for the fact that the Axis did not invade Malta. It resolves itself into this: We saw the odds were against us. We saw our need. We asked God for help and He gave it."

Among other Catholic papers, *The Catholic Transcript* of Hartford, Connecticut, printed the substance of the General's message as it was received through its news service.

One incident was picked up by a number of newpaper and published widely as an illustration of the tenacity of Dobbie's faith and the regard in which he held the teaching of the Word.

"One of the anecdotes told about him is of an incident when he was sent to quell the Arab-Jewish riots in Palestine in 1929. One of his officers remarked to another that this would be the easiest war ever fought.

" 'What do you mean by that?' the other inquired.

" 'We shall have to fight only four days each week. The Arabs will not fight on Friday, the Jews will not fight on Saturday, and Dobbie certainly will not fight on Sunday.' "

INCIDENTS AND ANECDOTES

As the Dobbie party went from the city to city, there were increasing evidences that the General was indeed touching the lives of men in high places. There is reason to believe that God used him in circles where few might have suspected that there was any real perception of eternal truths or realization of need for spiritual help.

It was more than once observed by Christians in some of the places visited, that figures of world importance felt free to consult Sir William in private after having heard him deliver a moving message on the reality of personal faith in God through His Son. What may have been discussed in those private conversations between outstanding leaders and this beloved man of God, could never be discovered from anything he said afterward. His very reticence was doubtless an invitation to some, to take advantage of the opportunity for spiritual counsel. His ministry touched those who would never have thought of consulting any of the familiar channels for securing light from the Scriptures upon their own needs.

So many of America's military leaders were present at functions where General Dobbie spoke that his ministry must have reached the hearts of many of them. In Tacoma, for example, 15 colonels and 3 generals sat at luncheon with him.

One story he told from the platform made a deep impression upon Christians among the military men who came to the meetings in his honor. A short time before Italy declared war on Great Britain, a telegram addressed to Dobbie was received from the Chief of the Imperial General Staff in England, a personal friend of the Governor, and the man who had asked him to take the post. It contained nothing except a Scripture reference, "Deuteronomy 3:22." Turning to the verse in the Bible, he read,

"Ye shall not fear them: for the Lord your God, He shall fight for you."

It is well known that England's leadership was permeated with a spirit of dependence upon God during the entire war. National days of prayer set apart by the King were followed by miracles of divine intervention. When any of Sir William's interviewers gave the impression that they thought his trust in God was unusual among Army men, he was quick to point out that there were many in the armed services who published abroad the fact that they were servants of Christ.

As Chairman of the Officers' Christian Union, the General had issued in tract form a notable document which came from a group of Admirals and Marshals of the British forces on land, on sea and in the air.

"The following statement has been signed by Commanders-in-Chief of the Royal Navy, Army, and Royal Air Force:

'We commend the gospel of Christ our Saviour, for it alone can effectively mould character, control conduct and solve the problems of men and nations.

'Faith in Christ the Lord, and loyal obedience to His will as revealed in the Bible, ensures peace of mind and brings satisfaction in service to God and man.'

Andrew Cunningham	B. Paget
Admiral of the Fleet	General
Jack C. Tovey	E. L. Gossage
Admiral of the Fleet	Air Marshal
H. R. Alexander	A. G. R. Garrod
Field Marshal	Air Marshal

Most of these names are familiar to Americans. They are all household names in Britain. Tovey is remembered as the man who sank the *Bismarck*. Alexander is almost as well known to the people of the United States as is Dobbie, for his prayer life, his use of the Bible in the orders he issued, and his early morning devotions.

If anyone tended to overemphasize Malta's importance in the Mediterranean theatre of operations, the General reminded them that without the brilliant Christian leadership of Alexander and Montgomery against Rommel, Malta's part in the conflict would have been in vain. He spoke in warm tones of Mongomery's love for the Scriptures, and his dependence upon the Lord in prayer for wisdom in the successful conduct of the campaign.

The meetings were not without their humorous side. In one immense building, a rather corpulent gentleman came to Sir William's side to guide him and Lady Dobbie through the crowded corridors to the speaker's platform. The General was heard to say to his wife, as they followed their guide,

"I say, Sybbie, it's jolly good to have a tank escort, isn't it?"

The "tank" ploughed through all opposition and successfully led the party to their objective.

In one meeting a cat somehow found its way to the platform. Dobbie related the incident to friends afterward at dinner.

"There I was, blissfully unaware that I was quite alone with the creature upon a great stage. It began to stalk me, but as it made ready to pounce, something frightened it away and saved my life. After that, my friends decided I should never be alone again, so someone was always present to guard me against the wild animals."

Usually the General, at his informal luncheon meetings, put his hearers at ease by opening his address with a story. Everyone was stiff and formal until he broke the ice with his dry humor.

"Our House of Lords corresponds in some measure to your Senate in Washington. I suppose you in America on

this account will appreciate the story of a certain member of
the House of Lords who was telling another about a dream
he had. 'I dreamed I was making a speech before our col-
leagues the other day. Then I wakened, and do you know,
I found out that I really was?'"

The laughter broke the tension and gave him a sympathetic hearing for the message which followed.

It was a privilege to hear Dobbie's conversation at the dinner table, as he relaxed with other Christians of the Moody
party. He related some strange things he had heard at prayer
meetings during his life in various corners of the earth. There
was the man who said, "Bless the gospel in the inhabited and
the uninhabited countries of the world, in this day when the
floodgates of infidelity and atheism are walking arm in arm
through the land." There was the speaker he had heard
using an unexpected series of metaphors, "I smell a rat. I see
it hovering in the air. I must nip it in the bud!"

Meeting Sir William was an experience long to be remembered. The author was much touched by the warm
hearted manner in which the General and Lady Dobbie responded to his questions about their earlier lives. A perfect
stranger had announced his need for biographical data for
the book which was to honor their visit to American shores
and perpetuate their ministry by setting the General's written
and spoken testimony for Christ before the people of the
United States.

The hundreds of newspaper articles which had been pe-
rused carefully before the interviews were to begin had created the impression that the General spoke only in monosyl-
lables. The word "taciturn" had been applied to him. One
news article had quoted Lady Dobbie as saying,

"You'll have to draw him out. He is positively inarticu-
late when it comes to speaking about himself."

Consequently, it was almost with fear and trembling that

questions were asked of the General about some of the details concerning the great gaps in the story of his life as it was generally known. The key to his heart was very evidently the Saviour who had dwelt there by faith for half a century. When it was understood that this was not an interview to satisfy idle public curiosity about a noted figure, but a sincere effort to glorify the Lord Jesus Christ through making known what He had done with one life which had been wholly dedicated to Him, Sir William frankly and fully answered every question.

He kindly overlooked any unintentional forgetfulness that here was one of the greatest men of the entire war. Sweeter fellowship in the Lord could not be found than one experienced with Sir William and Lady Dobbie. A more gracious and courteous pair would be hard to imagine.

When the first interview was over, an important mass meeting was scheduled within a short time afterwards. There was scarcely time to dress for dinner. Nevertheless, the General suggested,

"Let us have prayer together about these things."

In that hotel room, Sir William and Lady Dobbie knelt on the floor while he spoke simply, as though in the throne room of his God, and asked the Lord's blessing upon the writing of the present book. Especially did he ask that no man should be given undue prominence, nor brought between the reader and the Saviour of mankind. The writer confesses that he could scarcely refrain from showing how deeply touched he was upon hearing the General pouring out his heart for an unknown Christian. Seldom had he been brought as consciously into the presence of God as he was during that fervent, believing intercession. He knew something of the reason why it was that men who were with Dobbie on Malta afterwards spoke with reverent tones of the prayers which had been offered by the Governor in the palace of San Anton.

CANADA

In Canada the Inter Varsity Christian Fellowship became co-sponsor with the Moody Bible Institute of the Dobbie meetings. The General had long been interested in the work of the Fellowship in establishing a faithful Christian witness on the campuses of the universities of Canada and the United States. Therefore, Mr. C. Stacey Woods, General Secretary of the work, arranged meetings in Eastern Canada, and accompanied Sir William and Lady Dobbie on this part of their tour. Later the same plan was followed in the Western Provinces.

For some years the attendance at religious meetings of various kinds held in such centers of learning as the University of Toronto had been poor. When arrangements were being made for the General to address an evening convocation at the University, there was considerable apprehension lest the lack of interest prove embarrassing. Therefore, everyone was astonished to see the students crowding into the meeting place until the floor, the stairway and every other available space was filled. Hundreds were turned away.

This was found to be the experience of the Dobbie party all over Canada. The president of another university declared that the auditorium secured for the service was entirely too large, but his fears gave way to surprise when every seat was taken long before the hour announced for Sir William's message.

A typical meeting in one Canadian city found the doors open early, and every place in the building taken by 7:30 in the evening, although the scheduled time for the service was one hour later. It was necessary for the police to stand at nearby intersections to handle the crowds. Three thou-

A happy Maltese family.

Damaged homes near Grand Harbor.

The Governor of Malta reviewing
soldiers in training.

Loading British bombers on a
Malta airfield.

sand were turned away from that one place. This led to a
rather unexpected criticism of the Canadian tour. Although
Mr. Woods and the other men responsible for making
arrangements always insisted upon securing the largest auditorium available, letters appeared in the newspapers question-
ing whether something might not have been done to make
it possible for other thousands to enjoy the privilege of hearing the General's message. There were but two meetings
in all of the cities of Canada in which Sir William spoke,
where no one had to be turned away for the lack of room.

When the Western Provinces were visited, the only auditorium to be found in Vancouver, B. C., large enough to hold
the crowd was the City Forum, an ice arena. Since it was
found impossible to remove the ice for the occasion, a platform was built above it for the speakers. A band provided
by the Salvation Army was obliged to occupy chairs upon the
ice itself. When the newspapers reported the meeting, they
remarked that 5500 persons were on hand to witness the
"accidental symbolism" of Dobbie of Malta finding himself
upon another "island" of the British Empire, an island on
the ice, where he was surrounded by friends on every side,
rather than enemies.

In Victoria, B. C., after the largest military reception of
the entire tour, Sir William packed a theatre, while an over-
flow crowd filled a nearby Presbyterian church to which his
message was carried by a public address system. He made a
brief personal appearance to the latter audience afterward.
The hundreds who had been unable to see the film depict-
ing life on Malta during the bombings, persuaded the operator
to project it a second time for their benefit after the meeting
was over.

It was in Victoria that General Dobbie was invited to
open Canada's eighth war loan. Consistent with his firmly
held principles, he refused to do it on the Lord's Day, for

which tentative plans had been made, even though he might have included some reference to his Saviour in the ceremony. On the next day, however, he was happy to comply with the request of the government officials, by reviewing troops and formally opening the drive.

Queen Elizabeth had visited Toronto some time before the Dobbie tour. She had been honored in that city with the gift of a beautiful jewelled maple leaf on a background of silver, designed especially for her. When the Maltese League of Toronto desired to give the Lady Dobbie something unique as a token of appreciation for what she and her husband had done for Malta, it was learned that the original design for the maple leaf pin was still on hand. Those responsible for protocol gave their approval to the making of another similar piece of jewelry for Lady Dobbie, so that she became the only woman in the world besides the queen to possess such a jewel. The incident reveals how highly esteemed was the Dobbie visit to Canada.

The results of the Canadian meetings were everything that had been expected. A number of individuals made known to the party that they had come to a saving knowledge of Christ through the General's messages, in spite of the fact that no conventional evangelistic appeal was made. One such individual, although he wanted to reaffirm his faith rather than to receive Christ for the first time, brought more joy to the heart of Sir William than many an honor conferred by high officials.

A telephone call was received at the hotel in London, Ontario, where Dobbie was staying, by a member of the party who was seeking to make it possible for the General to get some needed rest. When the caller was asked if he could telephone at another time, he replied,

"Well, I should not want to disturb him. I owe him too much. I shall try to speak to him at a later hour."

"If you let me know who you are, and the nature of your business, perhaps I can help you."

"I am an Army man. I was a private at the time Sir William was stationed at Bermuda. He was just a subaltern then, but his quiet testimony on the boat and afterwards on the island brought me to know Christ as my own Saviour. He never knew what his witness had meant to me, but now that I see him still carrying on for his Lord after nearly forty years, I wanted to tell him about it."

The General was delighted to receive the man, as he always received with the utmost cordiality other Army men who sought him out for spiritual counsel. One such officer was a Roman Catholic, highly placed, who gave evidence of having come to a personal knowledge of the Lord through Dobbie's testimony in eastern Canada.

In McGill University the interest aroused by Dobbie's vigorous espousal of the gospel was so great that it became the subject most discussed by the faculty at subsequent weekly luncheons. Many students were visibly affected. Much comment was heard among them about the General's remarks.

Said the *Evangelical Christian,* "One of the most heartening things of the past five years has been the number of outstanding military leaders of Britain who have not been afraid to let it be known that their faith and hope is in God, and that they recognize their duty to God and their dependence on Him. That the British nation in these years of crisis should have been led by men of such outstanding faith and military skill is something for which we should as a people be grateful. That this nation was not overthrown in the swelling of Jordan when the floods of iniquity were loosed against us has been due in large measure to such Christian men as General Dobbie, Lord Gort, General Montgomery, and others."

Evangelical believers took notice that Sir William used at least five minutes to give a brief resume of the gospel everytime he spoke, no matter how short was the time at his disposal. He never failed to make it clear that man is a sinner needing a Saviour; that God has made His Son our Sin-bearer, and that all we need to do is to receive Him.

Churchmen who felt free to inquire about the General's views on the work of the church found that he emphatically stressed the importance of personal work as the key to church progress. He pointed out that the book of Acts indicates that worship, instruction, and fellowship are functions of the church as an organized body of believers, but that evangelism is a ministry to be carried out by individual Christians in their own vocations or professions. Dobbie's word to the churches of America was that when the modern church follows the example of the apostles, who went everywhere preaching the Word (Acts 8:4), apostolistic vigor and growth will be regained. If each member seeks to win others to Christ, instead of expecting the unsaved to come to a building to be evangelized by one man who carries the whole responsibility, then the church will grow in zeal and in numbers.

At the close of the eastern part of the Canadian tour, Mr. C. Stacey Woods summarized the meetings in a letter to Dr. Houghton. "I want you to know that, from an eternal point of view, a very great deal has been accomplished.

"General Dobbie himself spoke to well over 25,000 people, and Lady Dobbie to a very considerable number. I believe the majority of these people were young people, and a very great proportion of them were unconverted and unchurched.

"Perhaps the high-light of the tour was Ottawa, at which meeting the Governor-General read the Scripture lesson, and both Princess Alice and the Prime Minister were present. At the luncheon the next day in Chateau Laurier at which the leaders of the fighting services and the highest ranking cabinet ministers, including the three ministers of the army, air force, and navy, the Minister of Justice, etc., were present, the Prime Minister asked for the privilege of speaking, and those who have known him for many years said they have never seen him so moved. He spoke in a most amazing way about Calvary and the Saviour and our need of Christ. The same thing took place in the case of a couple of University Presidents.

"I do not think that it is too much to say that high Government and Academic circles have been stirred spiritually and challenged in a very personal way as has not taken place for perhaps a decade. It has been a most amazing experience. There have been a number of very definite conversions, for which we praise God.

"The entire visit, I believe, has been highly successful from every point of view. It has been a revelation to me as to the possibility of reaching the upper classes, and I hope that there may be further opportunities of this nature in the future.

"It has paid tremendous dividends to have taken the time and trouble in making initial contacts with those in high places. The newspaper publicity has been amazing. In three of our major papers there have been editorials about General Dobbie. Everything has been most faithfully reported."

Thus, in Canada, as in the United States, the audiences who heard Sir William's spoken testimony could be multiplied many times in the number who read his messages as they were reproduced in the daily press. As an editorial in the *Victoria Colonist* said, "The impression left by Sir William on his hearers was that of a conscientious servant of his country and his God, and so long as Great Britain retains within her service men of his noble type, she can neither faint nor fall."

PRESS REACTIONS

No one expected that the response of the American press to the visit of General and Lady Dobbie would be quite as enthusiastic as it turned out to be. Christian newspaper men were frankly surprised and pleased. Publicity agents attributed the tremendous crowds in large measure to the lengthy news items and splendid pictures which were spread over the dailies of every city included in the itinerary.

The files of the religious journals of England suggest the true reason why the Dobbie tour exceeded the expectations of so many. Commenting upon Sir William's departure from Britain, *The Life of Faith* said, "We are sure that his stirring testimony will be as greatly blessed in America as it has been throughout our own land." *The Christian* sounded a typical appeal for prayer, "The General and Lady Dobbie will appreciate the prayers of our readers that their testimony to the faithfulness of God may be divinely blessed to very many."

To the prayers of Christians in the British Empire were added the prayers of thousands throughout the United States and Canada, the result of a carefully planned campaign of publicity originating at the Institue of Chicago, and supported by the earnest petitions of the faculty, staff, and student body.

The nation-wide feeling of expectancy was expressed in the journal *Sunday*: "Speculation runs high today as to the possible results of the Moody-sponsored General Dobbie visit in America. Many authorities on evangelism have claimed that not since the days of D. L. Moody himself has any real appeal been made to the 'up and outers.'

"Moreover, they are inclined to admit that perhaps no one is better fitted to lead such a campaign today than Dr. Will H. Houghton of Moody. Hence, the combination of General Sir William and Lady Dobbie, under the direction of Dr. Houghton, looks like a real possibility."

After the distinguished visitors arrived, a London news-paper carried a cabled report of "the very favourable impression made by the General upon New York reporters, who besieged him last Sunday evening, with questions regarding the war situation. They expressed surprise at being greeted, not by a 'formidable brass hat,' but by a soft spoken gentleman who received them courteously and explained that he would sooner not discuss such matters on the Lord's Day. They instantly respected his wishes, and departed, with pleasurable anticipation of meeting him again on the morrow."

Even before Sir William had completed his earlier British tour, the magazine *Liberty* published an article on Dobbie by Donald Wilhelm which helped to prepare the way and introduce the General to America. Wrote Mr. Wilhelm: "This is the man who, more than any other, saved Malta. Quite possibly Malta saved Cairo, and conceivably it saved the war. In the grim days when Hitler was riding roughshod over Europe, some British politicians considered abandoning the little island outpost. It stood alone, a thousand miles from both Gibraltar and Alexandria and within twenty minutes of Axis flying fields on Sicily and in Southern Italy . . .

"Dobbie, of course, says he did little. He praised the people, and the garrison, the Royal Navy, the Merchant Navy, the Malta gunners, airmen, the Maltese, the wives, daughters, sisters of men in all the services. But many authorities in London and in Washington, and every one on the island itself from Governor Gort down, all say that, far more than any other man, Dobbie did the trick. He did it by his engineering skill, by his understanding of aviation, by making the most of the skills of many others—in a word, by personality and leadership. . .

"Dobbie is among the most thoroughly educated men in the British service . . . But it takes more than training or experience, to make a great leader. On his desk on Malta he had the text, 'If ye lack wisdom, ask of God.' "

That this wisdom was given, was evident to any who observed the significant fact that when the *Washington Post* carried its story of the General's visit to the Capital city, the adjoining column was headed, "Nazi Regime Plans to Leave Berlin." The man who had defied the Nazis in dependence upon the God of the Bible, was receiving public acclaim while his enemies who had defied the God of the Bible, were fleeing for their lives.

A biography could almost be written from the editorial and reportorial impressions of Sir William. A writer in a Louisville, Kentucky paper, was impressed by his stern subjection to God's will. "If Lieutenant General Sir William G. S. Dobbie, famous defender of Malta, had been born into another social circle, he could be pictured as the epitome of the stern, old-fashioned parent, undisputed ruler of his household, frowning on frivolity and bowing only to the will of God."

A reporter on the *New York Sun* discerned the spiritual as well, "His body is large and rugged looking, and his face is a blending of the stern and the spiritual, in the militant upward sweep of his bushy eyebrows and the gentleness of his deep-set blue eyes."

Said an editorial in *The Vancouver* (B.C.) *Daily Province*: "One could attribute to him in full measure Voltaire's praise of Marlborough, 'Calm courage in the midst of tumult,' and 'serenity of soul in the face of danger.' That serenity springs from deep convictions." Again, "General Dobbie is a man of military brilliance but he is also a pious man and a hard-working disciplinarian who has earned the title 'The Modern Gordon.' "

Beautifully timed with the height of the tour was George Creel's article in *Collier's,* in which he termed the General "a granite block of a man who joined military genius with the simple, unquestioning faith of an Old Testament prophet. When Italian bombs began to rain down without warning, his call for resistance to the death was sounded in the name of the Lord God of Hosts . . . Here was a member of the Plymouth Brethren, but the Maltese, although devout Catholics, followed him as though he wore a miter."

"The Faith of Dobbie of Malta," was the heading of a long article by columnist Judith Robinson in the Canadian papers, in which she quoted extensively the remarks of a soldier who had returned from Italy. He had much to say about "Dobbie, who had kept the Germans and Italians out of Malta by faith . . . Faith did it, old Dobbie's faith. All the troops in Africa knew that, and so did the fleet and the R.A.F." Even when the soldier got there in '42, "Africa was still full of stories about old Dobbie and how his drag with Omnipotence pulled Malta through . . . Sir William Dobbie believed, back in 1941, that the British peoples' usefulness to the Almighty was not ended, and that we could all be more useful to Him with Malta than without.

"Seems, if you have (his faith), you never have to worry about what's going to happen to you personally here below, because that doesn't matter. There's no future here. And you never have to worry about what will happen to your country or your people because the Maker of the Universe will look after them all right as long as they are being useful to Him in His long-term improvement plans. And if they stop being useful you don't have to worry either because what's the sense in any people being preserved if it is no longer of use to its Maker?"

The meeting in Harrisburg, Pennsylvania, drew typical editorials in the leading newspapers. Said the *News*: "Morale of a people at war could be no better stimulated than by the figure of a man who, against all the downward drag of war, resisted the tug and kept inviolate his religious vows. War plays havoc with the moral code. Under war's stress, men and women give way to actions alien to their better selves. Sir William Dobbie, along with other great military leaders of today and yesterday, demonstrates that there is something the impish hand of war cannot mar or master—the soul of a man reinforced by stout religious faith and convictions. Any man who reflects such a nature is worthy of respect and dependable for guidance."

Wrote the editor of the *Patriot,* "War has developed great heroes among the United Nations. Not all of them, however, are known as men of deep spiritual purpose. Sir William Dobbie shares with that other great English general, Bernard Montgomery, the reputation for never forgetting his God, no matter how heavily the bombs fell on his domain.

"In a conflict of human passion like war where the best and worst in men strive for mastery and where moral standards are so often forgotten or disregarded, it is inspiring to know that in this war there appears above the noise of cannon and curses the voice of a militantly religious leader of men whose comfort is in the Holy Book and whose faith rises to the stars.

"Wars normally do not breed religion, but Sir William Dobbie's case proves that war cannot kill religion either."

These are, of course, but samples of the impressive volume of favorable comment which appeared everywhere, greatly multiplying the good done by the ministry of this man of God. The significance of the tour was widely recognized. Said a news item about the General appearing in *United Evangelical Action*: "5,000 students recently convened in Hill Auditorium, University of Michigan, to hear Dobbie . . . Jointly sponsored by the Inter Varsity Fellowship chapter and the History Department, the convocation marked a significant event in campus evangelism in North America."

The Covenant Weekly commented about another gathering: "Seldom have we seen such an eager and attentive audience, and seldom have we heard such a gripping, yet simple message. As the tall, gray haired soldier faced his large audience of young people he seemed to take on some of the ruggedness of the island he so gallantly defended . . . As we cannot estimate the importance of his defense of Malta, neither can we calculate the importance of the simple testimony of this humble Christian soldier before his large American audiences."

A TYPICAL DAY

It was a fixed custom of many years' standing for Sir William to precede his daily work with an early morning period of private devotions. He esteemed God's Word above his necessary food in beginning each day. His comment was, "I have never found anything to compare with this morning watch as a source of blessing, when one meets God before meeting the world. It is a good thing to speak to Him before we speak to other people, to listen to His Word before we listen to the voices of our fellow men.

"Such a quiet time with the Word of God, when our minds are fresh, fortifies us to meet every problem and difficulty. Without it we are poorly prepared to begin our tasks. The Bible supplies us with food and strength enough to affect our well being throughout the entire day. However, breakfast is not the only meal provided for physical strength. Ordinarily we partake of three meals daily; likewise, we should feed upon God's Word several times. When we do this, we receive great stores of spiritual strength."

It made no difference where the General happened to be; break of day found him in communion with his God. On the train one of the men who accompanied Sir William and Lady Dobbie asked the porter to call him one morning at

seven o'clock, so that he could be ready to render any assistance needed before the breakfeast hour of eight. He was
awakened at 6:15 A. M. by the porter, who said, "You had
better get up now, sir. Your General is already up and
dressed."

It goes without saying that prayer was offered at meals,
whether the party sat down in a dining car or a hotel restaurant. It also is hardly necessary to state that while he was
no ascetic, Dobbie consistently refused the wine proffered at
governmental functions he was obliged to attend.

To a young Christian who asked whether such abstinence
did not adversely affect his army career, the General replied:
"To the contrary. More than once, I have had occasion to observe that when a small group of officers resolutely adhere to
their principles in refusing wine or liquor, they create an impression of strong mindedness among their superiors." With
Dobbie, there was no attitude of criticism or condemnation toward those who differed with him upon the subject. He re-
frained from using alcohol because he was honestly convinced
that he was pleasing Christ in so doing.

When reporters interviewed Sir William during the course
of the day, he managed to introduce enough of his personal
trust in the Lord to make certain the press reports would
carry something of definite witness afterward.

Every kind of question was asked of him. Why was Malta
saved? The General's answer was: "Because, in addition to
being the most bombed spot in the world, it was the most
prayed-for spot on earth. That is why it still lives today. I really believe that, aside from the King, we were most the prayed-
for people in the world. What a difference it made to know
that God's people in all parts of the world were praying
for us!"

Did the people of Britain turn to prayer because of the
war? "I am afraid not, to any large extent. Official days of

prayer bring many to church, but the bulk of the population does not seem to be seriously affected. However, there are without question many individuals who came to a personal knowledge of salvation as the result of the war."

Why did God permit World War II? "The war is God's way of speaking to the people of Britain as well as to those of other nations. Before the war many of them had forgotten Him, and since I witnessed the salvation of Malta, I feel it is my duty to bring this message everywhere I can."

Were the Allies right in expecting God to give them victory? "Yes. Our cause is righteous, and righteousness is the root of peace. I had faith in our cause in the last war and that faith has been confirmed by my experiences in this present conflict. Men who come through this war will realize more than ever that material things are not the only things in life. Our motto in the future must not be 'Peace at any price,' but, 'Righteousness at all costs.'"

Pastors of churches supporting the meetings asked about his favorite Scriptures. "The 46th and 27th Psalms greatly encouraged me when downhearted," he replied, "the latter seemed almost to have been written for us on Malta. We often thought also of Psalm 124:2,3, "If it had not been the Lord who was on our side, when men rose up against us: then they had swallowed us up quick, when their wrath was kindled against us."

How did the General determine the Lord's will? "You cannot hustle God. Wait quietly on Him. Go to bed, rise in the morning, and continue to trust in Him. Your mind makes itself up, as you go on sleeping, waking, praying, and working, so that you know what He wants you to do. He works in you 'both to will and to do his good pleasure.'"

What plan did he follow in reading the Bible? After becoming a member of the Officers' Christian Union at Woolwich, Sir William used the daily Bible readings which that organization publishes each year.

It meant much for him to know that in this way all of his friends in the Army around the world would be reading the same part of the Bible he was reading. In addition to these selected portions, he read three or more chapters of the Word consecutively every day, so that he completed the entire Bible each year. "Because of the hurly-burly of war," he loved the Old Testament, and especially the Psalms.

What was his favorite hymn? "It is found in *The Believer's Hymn Book*, and the first stanza goes,

"I'm waiting for Thee, Lord,
Thy beauty to see, Lord;
I'm waiting for Thee,
For Thy coming again."

Did this mean he believed the second coming of Christ was near? "The circumstances of the world are such," he replied, "that the coming of the Lord draweth nigh. This is a real hope, a solid hope. We who know Him may soon be taken up to meet those who have gone before."

Dobbie did not always wear his uniform, because he respected it as something which marked him as the representative of the king. He refused to permit it to become simply a spectacle for the curious to gaze upon. Therefore, when wearing it, he would eat nowhere except in the main dining room of his hotel, or at a luncheon in his honor at which members of the military were present. When in civilian clothes, he liked to hunt out some restaurant where he and Lady Dobbie might enjoy an unusual American dish in privacy.

Unfailing Christian courtesy characterized Sir William wherever he went. There was always something about a meal which was so good that he could thank the waiter for it. The room service was always so excellent in his judgment that he was able to thank the chamber maids on leaving a hotel.

There were four kinds of meetings in most cities: the business or professional men's luncheon, the University convocation, and the mass meeting, all addressed by the General, and the teas at which Lady Dobbie spoke. Observers believed Sir William's most impressive results were achieved at the luncheons, where a large percentage of the men usually were not professing Christians. Such gatherings were largely made up of civic and business leaders.

Invariably he set his audience at ease by a humorous anecdote. He was quick to seize upon anything in the introduction which might be turned to advantage in winning the sympathetic attention of the men. For example, he was introduced in one place by a gentleman who had been spoken of as famous for his golfing and his gardening. When the General began his address, he said,

"Our gracious host has been referred to as a well known golfer and gardener. They are two hobbies in which I also am interested. There is one notable difference between us, however. When I am golfing, the friends who are with me seem to think I am gardening instead."

The fact that he was not a preacher gave him unusual command of the interest of the men. After they became absorbed in his recounting of the battle of Malta, he would introduce the gospel in a perfectly natural way: "It is right and proper that we should pay our tribute to the work done by the defenders of the island. It is also superlatively right that we should pay tribute to God Himself, without Whom we never could have been spared. Just as God in the olden days helped those who asked Him, it is equally true today that He helps us in the present materialistic age in which we live.

"We learned certain lessons on the island. I think they are of value to both of our countries. First, we all pulled together, knowing that we must stand or fall together. We had a defense committee, consisting of the leaders of each of the services. We sat around a table and discussed each problem, not as a naval problem, nor an air force problem, but as a Malta problem.

"Gentlemen, we've got to face up to this. Cooperation must be achieved among the united nations, not merely lip service to it. There lies, humanly speaking, our hope for the future.

"The more important lesson is to be seen in the light of the fact that we were obviously inadequately garrisoned on Malta. But our human resources were not the only resources available. We put our trust in God. I do firmly believe, gentlemen, that therein lies the secret of the successful defense of the fortress. We could not win either the war or the peace, without the help of Almighty God.

"I want you to know that the things I am speaking to you about are very real and very practical, solid, hard facts. Faith in God is not something extra thrown in. It is the rock bottom thing. If we are going to help our country, we need to be on firm ground ourselves. It is no use trying to pull others out of the mud, if we are in the mud ourselves. May I tell you one little story to illustrate what I mean?

"In the Fall of 1917, my division was in Ypres. It was about October, and the weather had broken, so that the mud was like nothing on earth. One day I went up in the early morning to see the leading troops. After I had finished my business with them, I started to walk back. I was followed by my orderly, who walked a few steps behind me carrying a rifle.

"I came to a little hollow in the ground of which I thought nothing, until suddenly I found myself in the hollow of a bog. Right up to my waist in it I floundered, and I should have been there to this day had it not been for my orderly, who was a sensible fellow. He stopped where he was, on firm ground, and leaned forward and held out his rifle to me, and pulled me out, and here I am today. I noticed that he pointed the business end at me, but fortunately he did not have his hand on the trigger.

"He was able to help me because he was on firm ground. The only firm ground I know of is Jesus Christ, the Rock of Ages. He gave His life that He might redeem us. May I commend Him to you? He is the one your nation and mine needs."

Coming straight from the shoulder, such an appeal was bound to carry tremendous weight, especially when the one who made it wore the insignia of the crown and crossed swords, and the decorations with which his country had honored him.

The evening mass meetings were devoid of the "preliminaries" which have often been the curse of large gatherings centering in the address of a noted speaker. There was the singing of "The Star Spangled Banner," and as a courtesy to the distinguished guest of honor, a stanza of "God Save the King." A word from the chairman of the local committee which had arranged the service was followed by a brief prayer, and then the General, was introduced, usually by the Mayor, the Governor, or a university president. After a stirring sound film of life on Malta during a bombing attack, Sir William spoke.

The gathered thousands gave him their close attention as he recounted the experiences of the island during the siege. But when he neared the end of his discourse, and spoke of his Saviour, a hush of reverence rested upon the vast crowd. Something of the awe of God came upon the people as Sir William gave a ringing personal testimony for Christ, and a vigorous appeal that He be accorded His rightful place in the hearts and lives of his hearers.

He would tell of the day when he had accepted the Lord
Jesus as his Saviour, "on the terms that He had paid the
price of His shed blood in order that I might go free. I have
never been able for a moment to doubt that it was a real
transaction." About the Cross, he said, "With that ransom
God is fully satisfied, and I am too. Christ became not only
my Saviour, however. He became my Lord, and not only so,
but He has made Himself my Companion and my Friend.

"Ladies and gentlemen, I want to commend to you Jesus
Christ. I have proved Him, experienced His friendship and
companionship throughout life. I give you what may be called first hand evidence. If we have Him, we can face anything.
If we open our hearts to Him, then He will make our lives
what they ought to be, and then we shall be able to help our
country, which we long to do. We, and the nations to which
we belong, must recognize that without God's help we cannot win through these difficult years, but that with His help,
we can."

EVALUATING THE TOUR

It would be an impossible task to evaluate the results of
the Dobbie tour in terms of the number reached for Christ,
great as it undoubtedly was. There are too many other factors which loom large in the thinking of those who have considered this amazing ministry in its broad perspective.

As Sir William and Lady Dobbie went up and down the
land, visiting some 40 cities, traveling a total of 15,000 miles,
and addressing at least 150,000 people, it was repeatedly observed by Christian leaders everywhere that God was evidently doing a mighty work through the various meetings.
The publicity given to the messages and views of the titled
pair greatly enlarged their witness, so that the actual number
in attendance at the services was but a fraction of the multitudes reached by radio, newspaper, magazine, and tract.

The technique of the tour was such that it was not found wise to make an evangelistic appeal everywhere. It was the General's earnest belief that since salvation is of the Lord, it would be better for those who had found Christ to look back to a personal transaction with Him, than to an outward religious act which might have been the result of emotion rather than the regenerating work of the Holy Spirit. However, the pulse of the services was taken in one gathering of young people, where the leader of the local committee had prepared decision blanks to be signed by all who received the Lord as a result of Sir William's message. Forty nine names were turned in at the close of that meeting.

Voluntary testimonies to the saving power of Christ were numerous, from people who were born again at meetings in various parts of the country. Generals and other army officers, mayors, and outstanding leaders in governmental and professional circles, sought out Sir William for private consultation on spiritual matters. There is no question that his spiritual impact upon people in high places was tremendous.

The Moody Bible Institute found it necessary to turn down hundreds of urgent requests for meetings which simply could not be included in a four months' itinerary. By letter, by telegram, by long distance telephone, and by personal representative, Christians literally pleaded for an opportunity to bring General Dobbie before their communities. They declared the interest was so great that it was certain the largest auditoriums would be filled to capacity when he spoke.

An examination of the correspondence with these hundreds of cities makes it clear that the tour has led to the discovery of a far greater need for the kind of ministry the General represented, than he could have filled in more than two years. There is no reason to doubt that his visit will result in an emphasis upon what amounts to a new form of evangelism designed to reach the leaders of American life, by which Christ and Him crucified may be brought to the attention of those who have not been touched by older, conventional methods of proclaiming the gospel.

It has not always been possible to bring together various Christian groups in support of united campaigns for mass evangelism. Personalities, doctrinal differences, old prejudices, and other hindrances have not been easy to overcome. It is commonly admitted that evangelism of the type so greatly owned of God in the days of D. L. Moody, has steadily declined since his time. Whatever may have been the reason, General Dobbie's visit brought people together under the sound of the gospel in such a way as to encourage local committees to hope for other successful gatherings in the future.

Undoubtedly, there were international benefits derived from the tour, because Christians in America were drawn closer to believers in the British Isles, through Sir William's and Lady Dobbie's ministry, than they had been in a generation. From the largest gathering of 9,000 in Minneapolis, to the smallest luncheon; from the universities of the Pacific coast to those of New England and Canada; from Tacoma's crowded theater meeting to Boston's Park Street Church service, the British visitors endeared themselves to the hearts of the American people.

Army men throughout the trip heard in language they could understand, the Christian witness of a man recognized as a great soldier whose ability and bravery were beyond question. They wrote in *The Armored News,* official army organ of the Fort Knox post: " 'We cannot win in this war, or in peace,' has been the General's message, 'without God's help. Human resources and human efforts, however great, are not enough. To gain His help we must be fit to receive it. This involves ruthlessly putting away those things which we know are displeasing to Him, confessing our sins, and turning from them.' " Two thousand navy personnel listened to similar outspoken words, as they gathered in Princeton, N. J., near the end of Sir William's ministry.

University students and faculty members found in the cultured speeches delivered on their campuses an effective antidote to prevailing skepticism and godlessness. The hands of evangelical agencies seeking to reach college age youth were strengthened and encouraged. An unknown number of young people were led to devote their lives to serving Christ in whatever way they could. Everyone partook to some degree of the feelings of the man who wrote to a London paper after hearing Dobbie speak to the people of Malta, "General Dobbie's broadcast words of encouragement were a source of inspiration to all. Least of all, shall we ever forget his words, 'With God's help we shall win.' "

On the way East from California, the General and his wife spent a short time in Chicago, during which they addressed a farewell chapel service at the Moody Institute. Lady Dobbie mentioned the fact that her text for the tour had been, "As thy days, so shall thy strength be" (Deut. 33:25). The verse kept coming to mind as the long train rides, the strain of meeting many new people each day, the frequent platform appearances, and other trying experiences incidental to such an undertaking, threatened to overtax them physically. "But," she asked, "how could God give one a job to do, and not give the strength for it?"

She pointed out that one evident token of the blessing of God upon them, in answer to the prayers of the Institute family and friends, was the absence of broken engagements. They had always been well and strong enough to be present at every meeting. Taxicabs might have broken down, trains might have been too long delayed, or sickness might have overtaken one of them, but the Lord preserved them from every such eventuality.

Lady Dobbie confessed to having sometimes faced her American audiences with fear and trembling because they were so much larger than the women's groups to which she had been accustomed in England. "The Lord had evidently chosen me to speak for Him. I did not know why, but I knew I must go at His bidding. I went to each meeting knowing I had nothing to attract people except the fact that I am the wife of my husband."

She used the figure of a nail being driven into a piece of wood, as an illustration of what they, and other instruments whom the Lord might be pleased to use, tried to do in bringing the knowledge of salvation to others.

"Someone places the nail in position by speaking to an individual about Christ as Saviour for the first time. Perhaps this is a mother, or a friend, or a Sunday School teacher. It may have little apparent effect. Then others, as time passes, each strike that nail a blow, and drive it in a bit farther, with a word is season about the Lord. Finally someone, perhaps an evangelist, happens to strike the final blow, and the individual is saved. That last person is likely to think he has done a great work, and indeed he has, but he has really done no more than any of the others, each of whom has played a part in winning the other to Christ.

"That is what we have been doing, trying to strike the nail on the head to the best of our ability. We have not concerned ourselves with results, leaving all that with the Lord. We hope that there have been cases where some heard about Christ for the first time, so that the nail has been started which will be driven all the way in by others in the future. It has been a real privilege to add our testimony to that of the Christians who preceded us."

Sir William's final message to the Institute was introduced by the reading of Acts 14:24-27. He then freely rendered the passage in applying it to his American tour. "And after they had passed through British Columbia, they came to Seattle. And when they had preached the Word there, they went down into California. And thence they took a train to Chicago, from whence they had been recommended to the grace of God for the work which they fulfilled. And when they were come, and had gathered the church together, they rehearsed all that God had done for them."

The General said: "We speak not of what we have done, but of what God has done. We have had a wonderfully happy time. We have had wonderful privileges. We have been amazed all through by the opportunities given us and staggered by them from time to time. We desire to thank you for the way you have upheld us in prayer.

"The whole object of every meeting was to present Christ. We have been extraordinarily well received. There never were any unkind words. As we faced large crowds, and looked at those thousands with urgent needs which only Christ could meet, we were reminded of how our Lord was moved with compassion when he saw the multitudes.

"Another feeling I had some times. Seeing the tremendous opportunities, I felt like a member of the armed forces. Those in command had arranged a certain set of plans, but the opportunity facing the army would fail unless the humble soldier did his part. The Lord had placed me in this position to take advantage of it to the fullest. I had an overwhelming feeling of responsibility to make the most of the chance of speaking to those vast audiences of influential people. Please continue praying that Christ will indeed bless the work which He has begun in many hearts and bring it to perfection."

When Sir William and Lady Dobbie left Chicago for the last part of their tour in the East before sailing for England, they were completing an itinerary which had taken them through much of the United States and Canada. From New York, where they had arrived on the *Queen Mary* on Jan-

uary 19, 1945, they had gone via Washington to the Middle
West, through the cities of eastern Canada, Pennsylvania and
Maryland to Kentucky and Tennessee. After visiting St.
Louis, Kansas City, and other cities of the Mississippi River
valley, they had passed through western Canada to the metro-
politan areas of Washington, Oregon, and California.

The last "Youth for Christ" mass meeting addressed by
Dobbie was held in the Boston Opera House, where the Governor of Massachusetts introduced the General to 3,000 young
people assembled for the first religious service ever held in
that building. Appearances before various business men's or-
ganizations were followed by the final meeting of the eastern
conference of the Moody Bible Institute at Carnegie Hall,
New York City. The tour ended when Sir William spoke to
a small select group of Christians at the famous Wayside
Inn of Sudbury, Massachusetts, immortalized by Longfellow
in his "Tales of a Wayside Inn."

The quietness of this leave taking seemed most fitting as
the climax of the ministry of one whose humility had so deeply impressed his audiences all over America. However, the
true greatness of the man was once more emphasized, in
spite of his own modesty, when steamship officials arranged
for him to return to Europe on the *Queen Mary,* pride of the
British merchant fleet.

The General and his gracious Lady sailed on June 5, 1945.
All who knew them were genuinely sorry to see them go.
They went back to an England where victory had come since
their departure nearly five months before. It was a victory in
which they had played no small part, during the days when
their nation had been upon the brink of catastrophe. And it
was a victory symbolic of the faith of Dobbie of Malta, expressed five years before, when he had faced the desperate
plight of his island with the immortal words, "We may have
to suffer, but with the help of Almighty God, we shall win!"

III
THE MESSAGE

A Collection of Addresses and Articles

GENERAL DOBBIE'S PERSONAL TESTIMONY

An address given in London

IT is a very good thing that we do not have to talk about ourselves. It would be a dreadful thing if we had—dreadful for us, and dreadful for you. What we have to talk about is One who has made all the difference in our lives—the Lord Jesus Christ. I stand here to tell you what the Lord Jesus has been to me.

I came to Christ and trusted Him as my Saviour when I was a boy at Charterhouse School, getting on to fifty years ago. It came to me in this way. I felt the burden of my sin. Even boys can feel that, and I certainly did. And that burden was a very grievous burden to me.

One Sunday evening I suddenly realized that He had died in order to put away my sins, and to blot them out. And God, for Christ's sake, that evening did forgive me my sins, and blotted them out; and I have known ever since that all my sins—even those which I have committed since then, and they have been many—have all of them been put away once and for all.

I could not doubt that, because it depends upon what He did and not upon what I have done. I am never tired of saying, am I am glad of this opportunity to say so once again publicly, that I owe everything to Him, "who loved me, and gave himself for me." He has dealt with the question of the past; He has blotted it out.

He deals with the question of the present. He keeps us and helps us in all sorts of circumstances. In all the vicissitudes of Army life, I have found that He is able to keep and to help. I have tried Him in peace and in war; I have tried

Him in all sorts of circumstances, and never once has He failed. And I am now speaking of a period that is getting on to fifty years.

It would be a poor thing to be in the Army if you were not a Christian. I would like to say that from the bottom of my heart. I would not dream of facing life in the Army, or out of it, without Christ. I do not know how people can go on trying to live without Him, especially in these troublous and anxious days in which we live.

Many of you here, I know, have prayed for me in these last few years when I was abroad. I want to thank you for having done so, and to tell you how very greatly my wife and I valued your prayers, and what a difference it made to us to know that God's people in all parts of the world were praying for us.

I really believe that, perhaps apart from the King, we were the most prayed-for people in the world, and it meant more to us than I can say. Many times, when things have been difficult, we have talked to each other, and we have said: "Remember all the people who are praying for us," and it has been a tremendous help. I wish to thank you from the bottom of my heart for what you have done.

One of the things which has been on my mind in the last year or two is the subject in which many are especially interested—that is, the return of our Lord. When one sees the world in the terrible mess in which it now finds iteslf, one longs all the more for that return of our Lord. Personally, I verily believe that He will come soon. I think so. What I have felt more and more in this last year or two is how necessary it is for us Christians to lessen our connections with this world, and to dwell in the heavenly places; for where our treasure is, there will our hearts be also.

It has been a great help to me to read such verses as those in the twelfth chapter of Romans telling us not to be conformed to this world, but to be transformed; to have our affections set on things above, and not on the things of the earth. We have set before us a wonderful hope. The Lord's return is the hope which has meant so much to us. And, as these difficult days come and pass, it means all the more to us.

That is the wonderful hope which was before us in Malta. I was constantly thinking of it; and although there are many things in connection with His coming which may be difficult to understand, and about which I would not dare to dogmatize, yet we have His definite promise that He will come again to reign on this earth, and to put things right which cannot be put right in any other way. That is something which has meant a tremendous lot in the rough-and-tumble of the life which we have had to live.

My time has practically come to an end. Again I want to say that I owe everything to the Lord Jesus Christ, who has saved me from the guilt of sin. He has kept me from its power, and He has helped me in a very practical and real way through these many years of Army life. It is a really practical thing to put one's trust in the living Christ, and to come to God by Him. I commend that Saviour to you, and especially to my comrades in the Services who are here to-night, so that they may find in Him, as I know they will, if they will give Him a chance, exactly what I have found, and possibly more still.

WHAT I BELIEVE

A Radio Message given by General Dobbie at the request of the British Broadcasting Company.

It is necessary not only to enunciate the beliefs one holds in the things which cut deepest, but it is also very desirable to consider the reasons for these beliefs and to be clear about the foundation on which they rest. Before answering the question, "What do I believe?" I therefore propose to say a

few words about the foundation on which my beliefs rest, so
that the value of the conclusions reached may be rightly as-
sessed.

It is, of course, easy for anyone with an agile mind to in-
vent the most wonderful beliefs, but they will, I fancy, give
him little help and satisfaction as he faces the problems of
life, and will certainly count very little with others, if they
are simply the product of his imagination and nothing more.
But if one can find a real and sure foundation, outside and
superior to the human mind, whether one's own mind or that
of other men, then one can have the confidence and assurance which we all desire, and it will act as a firm anchor in
all the changing circumstances of life.

I am convinced that such a foundation can be found, and
that millions all down the centuries have found it in the inspired Word of God, the Holy Scriptures of the Old and New
Testaments, commonly known as the Bible. That seems to
me to be the one and only sure foundation on which we
can with confidence build our beliefs and hopes. It has the
authority of God Himself, and tells us with all the force of
that authority what Almighty God thinks about the deepest
things of life, things which are beyond the power of the
human mind to understand and master. It is possible that
some of the things which He tells us in His Book may run
counter to our natural ideas and instincts. It would be surprising if that were not so, but in such cases it will surely be
incredibly foolish of us if we on our part persist in pitting
our puny intellects against the wisdom of the Maker of the
universe, a wisdom which He Himself tells us is inconceivably
higher than ours.

It is, therefore, on this basis that I venture with all humility
to set out very briefly and simply some of the things which
I find He says to us in His Book and which form the basis
of my belief.

I BELIEVE that God intended that man should be for His (God's) own delight and pleasure, and that man for his part should be able to enjoy God's presence and companionship. But I find that this purpose was frustrated by the Fall, when sin entered in and formed a barrier between man and God. I find that God planned to remove this barrier by dealing with the sin of man, and deliver man from its guilt and penalty.

I BELIEVE that it was for this precise purpose that the Son of God, whom we know as the Lord Jesus Christ, came to this earth, and offered Himself as a sacrifice in order to pay the penalty for our sins and thus to reconcile us to God.

I BELIEVE that by this sacrifice the righteous claims of God were fully met, and that in consequence we may go free.

I BELIEVE that on the ground of this sacrifice, and on no other ground, God for Christ's sake does forgive our sins, and that we may become in a very real sense children of God through faith in Jesus Christ.

I BELIEVE that as a result we may enjoy, here and now, all the unspeakable advantages and privileges of that relationship; that we may experience and enjoy in a very real and practical sense the companionship and friendship of the Lord Jesus Christ.

I BELIEVE that we can count on His help in all the problems of life, whether they are great or small, and whether they are concerned with our official and professional life or with our private affairs.

I BELIEVE that we can take all these problems to Him in prayer at any time and in any place, and can expect to receive from Him the wisdom and help needed to deal with them.

I BELIEVE that in addition to these things, He gives us power to overcome sin in our daily life—the sin which otherwise is too strong for us, and which spoils, in fact ruins, our lives.

I BELIEVE that He gives us this power so that nothing need intervene which would interrupt our constant enjoyment of His companionship, and in order that we may be able to carry out His commands to live pure and useful lives and reach out to His standard.

I BELIEVE that in view of all He has done for us, in loving us and giving Himself for us, He expects us in return to give Him our love and our allegiance, and to make Him our Lord and Master, and to obey Him, follow Him, serve Him, and try to please Him in everything, and, in a word, to put Him in the first place in our lives.

I BELIEVE that He calls upon us to acknowledge and own Him and be faithful to Him even when, or especially where, He is not acknowledged or owned by others around; because He condescends to acknowledge and own us.

I BELIEVE that He is the only solution for our problems and our needs, whether individual, national, or international; that all the plans we make in these various spheres can only be successful in so far as He is allowed to control them.

I BELIEVE that He, and He alone, is able to solve and put right the immense difficulties with which this world of ours is faced, and that He will ultimately assume direct control in order to do so.

I BELIEVE that all the purposes of God for this world, which are unfolding before our eyes, are directed towards this same end—the reign of Christ on earth.

Most of what I have said refers to the relationship between God and man, but I find also God requires that man's relationship with man should be put upon a proper basis, and that man should love his neighbor as himself, and that the dealings between man and man should be based on love, unselfishness, kindness, and the like. Further, I find that the latter, man's relationship with man, can never be put right unless and until man's relationship to God is put right first. The other will then follow automatically.

The foregoing beliefs which I have enunciated are based upon what I read in Holy Writ. They are stated therein in clear and simple language; each of these beliefs can be easily substantiated from God's Word. For that reason, I maintain that they form a reliable foundation on which to build. But, in addition to that basis, I would add, in conclusion, that in so far especially as they have to do with the individual life, I have found that my experience is entirely in line with what is written in the Bible. I have found that the assurance of sins forgiven for Christ's sake is very real, that His help, companionship, and friendship are very real; that the help He gives to overcome sin is very real; that intercourse with Him through prayer or the reading of His Book is very real and practical, and that the Christian life, if it is lived in dependence on and in obedience to Him, is a very feasible, practical, and happy thing.

UNDER SCRUTINY OF FRIEND AND FOE
Written for *Practical Christianity*, organ
of the Officers' Christian Union

One sometimes hears it said: "If . . . is a Christian, then I will have nothing to do with Christianity." This is, of course, a childish argument, and is really rather an excuse for continuing to live without God, than a valid reason for so doing. One might as well say: "There are spurious pound notes going about. I met one the other day; therefore I will have nothing to do with pound notes any more!"

It is, however, a terrible dishonor on the name of Christ and a disgrace to us, who profess to bear His name, that such a thing could even be said, whatever the motive may have been. We have got to see to it that it can never justly be

said of us. It is not enough to take it for granted that of
course it could not be said of us. No, we have got to get to
it, and "examine ourselves," and go through our lives with
meticulous care so as to insure that nothing has slipped in
which may cause offence to "weaker brethren" or repel anyone from Christ.

What is more, we have got to let God examine us with
His all-seeing and holy eye to "see if there be any wicked
way" in us. After all, in the case of many persons with whom
we come in contact, all that they know or learn of Christ is
what they see in us. They perhaps do not bother to read Bibles
—but they read us, and they probably do so far more closely
than we imagine.

David apparently realized this. He asked God, "Lead me
in Thy righteousness because of those who observe me" (mar-
ginal reading of Psalms 5:8 and 27:11). It is all important and
must be our constant concern that we give a true picture of
Christ and not a caricature.

It involves taking trouble, since it cannot be achieved
otherwise. Paul said, "Herein do I exercise myself (take
trouble), to have always a conscience void of offence toward
God, and toward men" (Acts 24:16). Peter said we must be
"diligent" in the matter. No, it is not easily insured, nor can
we insure it by our own human efforts alone; but the grace
of God and His power can do the impossible. Our part is to
be in dead earnest about it.

The quotation above from Acts 24:16, is significant. There
are two sides to the question, the God-ward and the man-
ward. It is significant that Paul puts the God-ward side first.
If God can look into our lives, and see in them nothing which
is displeasing to Him, man will not be able to find anything
about which he can justly find fault. Men may, of course,
find fault, but in that case the circumstances to which the
Lord referred in Matthew 5:11, would seem to apply, for men

would then be saying evil things against us "falsely for Christ's sake."

Let us be sure that, if evil things are said against us, they are not said because of any lack of the Christian graces in us, or because of any wrong action on our part. Peter was alive to this danger when he warned Christians against it, "If ye be reproached for the name of Christ, happy are ye; . . . But let none of you suffer . . . as evil-doer, or as a busybody in other men's matters" (I Peter 4:14-16).

Our lives must bear scrutiny on the part of God and man, and if they are to pass muster under this scrutiny, Christ must live in us—not intermittently, but constantly. Can this be done? It must be possible, since God never gives an impossible order. Rather, when He gives an order He also provides the means whereby the order may be carried out in its entirety. He is willing to give us that constant renewing and replenishment which we need, and by "renewing a right spirit within us" He can "create and maintain in us a clean heart." This is what David sought and found in Psalm 51:10.

This was Paul's experience when he said "the inward man is renewed day by day." Paul's remark, or rather, the Holy Spirit's word through Paul, recorded in Philippians 1:10, is significant. He exhorted the Christians to be "sincere and without offence till the day of Christ." These expressions remind us of the statement he made before Felix which we have already noticed. The word translated "sincere" is a remarkable one. The meaning of it as given in the Greek Dictionary is "that which, being viewed in the sunshine, is found clear and pure."

This surely corresponds to the "conscience void of offence toward God" at which he aimed. But what a standard it is! It comprises not only the deed done or the word spoken but also, and perhaps chiefly, the motive behind it! That is a thing which only God can see. Man may see the outward result, but God looks into the heart, and discerns its "thoughts and intents," so that everything is laid bare "before the eyes of him with whom we have to do."

We can now enter into the Psalmist's feelings when he said, "O Lord, thou hast searched me and known me . . . Thou understandest my thought afar off" (Psa. 139:1,2). We do well to ponder this matter, and ask God not only to search us, but to cleanse us and indwell us. Thus only can we face that scrutiny of the "sunlight," and be found clear and pure.

But Paul also tells the Philippians to be "without offence." This would seem to correspond to the "conscience void of offence toward men." In this connection he warns us also to "abstain from all appearance of evil" so that we may neither cause offence nor make some stumble who may be weak in the faith, nor hinder others from coming to Christ. This may involve a measure of unselfishness on our part. If we hesitate to make any little sacrifice that may be involved, let us remind ourselves of what Christ gave up for us, and of the sacrifice He made. We will then hesitate no longer.

Paul tells us that this attitude toward God and men is to be maintained "till the day of Christ." What we have been considering is not to be an isolated act, nor a series of such acts. It is to be a permanent condition, brought about by Christ living in us, and showing Himself in all departments of our life. We may remind ourselves again that such a state is not easily attained or maintained. It needs diligence, earnestness, and love to Him. But it is surely worth the effort, because by this means, and this means alone, will men "see our good works and glorify our Father." May God help us all who name the name of Christ to be in earnest about these things and allow Him to work in us "both to will and to do of His good pleasure."

THE NEED OF A NATIONAL CHANGE OF HEART
An address given in England
on the eve of a National Day
of Prayer in 1942.

I feel it to be a very great responsibility to be standing here this evening in front of you, and speaking to you, seeking to set the tone to this great and important gathering. I am very conscious of my own weakness and unworthiness for this task; and I want at the outset of my remarks to read you two verses from the Book of Daniel (9:18, 19): "O my God, incline thine ear, and hear; open thine eyes, and behold our desolations, and the city which is called by thy name: for we do not present our supplications before thee for our righteousnesses, but for thy great mercies. O Lord, hear; O Lord, forgive; O Lord, hearken and do; defer not, for Thine own sake, O my God: for thy city and thy people are called by thy name."

"O Lord, hear; O Lord, forgive . . . . for we do not present our supplications before thee for our righteousnesses"— not even because the cause which has been committed to us is outstandingly righteous either. Many of us are, perhaps, troubled and puzzled by certain questions which are bound to arise in our minds on an occasion like this, at the time of the National Day of Prayer.

Three years have gone since war was declared; three years of untold trouble, and sorrow, and misery to the whole world; and the war goes on. And we are troubled — very naturally, perhaps—by certain questions which arise in our minds. I am going to mention those questions to see if we can answer them.

One question is: Can God deliver? Well, we know the answer to that, don't we? We know that He can. We have seen His delivering hand at work many times over during this war in a most marked way that leaves us in no doubt at all. We saw it in a very marked way also in the last war. Go back in thought to the last war. It was a very remarkable thing to see the way that God, for the four years of that war, withheld success from us. On many occasions we were within an ace of success, but we did not get it until the end. And, on other occasions, we were within an ace of disaster, but God delivered us.

It looked as if He were withholding success until we, as a nation, approached Him in the right way, and acknowledged our need of Him; and we did that, for the first time, by order of the Government, on the 4th day of August, 1918; and after that, everything went successfully. There was no looking back; things were far more successful than most of us ventured to think, or dared to hope, at that time.

God did intervene, and God did deliver us when we acknowledged our need of Him, as we did on that 4th day of August, 1918. So the answer to that first question, can God deliver? is, He most certainly can, because we have seen Him doing it, and history is full of instances which are recorded for our encouragement and learning, that God can and does deliver those who put their trust in Him.

If that is so, the next question is this: Why does not God give us the deliverance we are so much longing for, and praying for? There have been gatherings like this in this hall every month since the war started, in which prayer has been made to God that in His great mercy He would intervene, and help us, and give us the victory.

We are sure that our cause is definitely a righteous one. The war was forced upon us; we did not choose it for any purposes of our own—it was thrust upon us; and we know that ours is a righteous cause. There can be no doubt about that. We are puzzled, also, as to why God allows those who are our enemies, so flagrantly to defy Him, as they do. We wonder why He allows that; why He does not strike them down.

All these things puzzle us. We Christian people who have been praying for so long know that our cause is righteous, and that our enemies have been flaunting defiance in the face of Almighty God, and we ask the question: Why does not God grant us deliverance? But don't you think that wars, like other judgments of God, are sent, or are allowed, in order to teach us something we cannot, or will not, learn in any other way?

I, personally, am convinced that God is speaking to us through this war in order to bring us as a nation to a right attitude of mind toward Him—and, remember, the nation is made up of individuals. Our attitude, as a nation, toward God has not been God-honoring. God is not put in His right place; and God is speaking to us by means of these troubles that He has allowed to come to us. He is speaking to us loudly and clearly and telling us to put right our attitude toward Him.

We are ignoring Him; we are indifferent to Him; we think that we can, by our own efforts, win the victory. But we cannot do so. One sees posters pasted up on the boardings, and one hears the slogans: "*Your* determination, *Your* endurance, *Your* courage, *Your* efforts, will win us the victory." That is only partially true. Those things are, of course, needed, but the thing which matters more than anything else is a realization of the fact that victory is the gift of Almighty God, who alone is the Arbiter in human affairs. We have to learn that lesson as a nation; and I believe that God is trying to get us to learn it, in His great mercy.

He has from time to time, during this war, given us wonderful and signal deliverances. We have thought about them—at the time of the evacuation of our troops from the continent in the early summer of 1940, and at the time of the

Battle of Britain later on, and on other occasions. He has delivered us from disaster, and yet He has, so far, withheld success from us.

He is seeking from us that we should alter our attitude toward Him, as a nation, and put Him in His rightful place. It is not enough, as some people might think, on these special Days of Prayer that are called for from time to time when the situation is difficult; it is not enough just to turn to God, and to implore Him to help us because of our great anxieties and perplexities. That is a sort of "emergency religion," as I have heard it called.

That is not what God is looking for. He is looking for a change of heart, a change of mind toward Him, so that He may be able to give us the blessings which He is longing to give. It is not just the case of an "emergency religion" when we find ourselves in difficulties. We need a change of heart. It is not a case of turning to God in a patronizing way to ask Him to come and help us. He is calling upon us as a nation to change our attitude of mind and heart toward Him. This is the literal meaning of the Greek word translated in our Bibles as "repentance"; and God is calling us to repentance.

I was very much struck when I was reading this passage the other day about Daniel, who was a good man if anyone was, how he felt it necessary to repent also. This is what he says: "While I was speaking, and praying, and confessing my sin and the sin of my people Israel, and presenting my supplication before the Lord my God. . . ."

It does not do for us to think how that the rest of the people need to repent. What about you and me? We have got to take our share of the national attitude toward God. If we had been more faithful, and if we had followed Him more closely, the attitude of the nation toward God might have been different. We cannot get out of that responsibility.

We, as Christian people, must confess our sins, just as the nation confesses its national sins.

Until we do so we are hindering God from giving us the blessing which I believe He is longing to give. We are doing a very great disservice to our country—and that is putting it on a level which is not a very high one—since, by our individual and national indifference toward God, He is being hindered from giving us the victory for which we long.

Well now, God is speaking to us, and I think the burden of our prayer ought to be, not so much that He will give us the victory, but that rather He will enable us as a people to remove the obstacles which are in the way of His granting us the blessing which He longs to give. It rests with us; it rests with our nation to turn to Him and to acknowledge our need of Him—to acknowledge that we cannot succeed apart from His help. And even if we did win the war, we would make an awful mess of the peace if our attitude toward Him was not right.

We want to acknowledge not only our national sins, but our personal sins, and to turn from them in repentance. If we do that, I believe that God will, in a most wonderful and striking way, intervene and grant us His blessing. May God help our nation at this solemn time to hear His voice speaking to our people, and to hearken, and to obey, and to do the task which He has committed unto us.

WHAT THE BIBLE MEANS TO ME
An Address delivered before the
Scottish National Bible
Society, Edinburgh

I would like to tell you what the Bible is and has been to me during these many years since I first came to love it and to read it. It has meant a tremendous lot to me, and perhaps I might confine my remarks on this matter mainly to what it has been to me in these last two years when I had a very happy and memorable period, and when, in God's great goodness, His Word to me fully met my needs.

I personally find the Bible of value to me in various ways. May I tell you one or two of them, and I think that you will agree with me that it is the same to you. For one thing, God's Word, His inspired Word, the Bible, tells me what God thinks about certain vital and deep things. It does not really matter to us what man thinks about them. It matters but little really, but what does matter is that we should be able to know what God thinks, so that we should be able to look at things through His eyes and see things in their right perspective. The Bible itself tells us that God's thoughts are very different from our thoughts, and we, not unnaturally, find as we read it that some of the things He tells us that He thinks, are very different from what our natural minds think about these things. But it is good that we should know what God thinks about them, and that is one reason why I value God's Book.

Another thing that the Bible does for me is that it tells me about the Lord Jesus Christ. If it were not for this Book, the inspired Word of God, we would not know what He has done for us, and we would not know what He is prepared to do for us day by day in our lives. If it were not for this Book we would not know the real meaning of God's edicts, or the sacrifice on Calvary; we would not know the true significance of the Resurrection; we would not know the meaning of the Ascension, and the coming of the Holy Spirit into the world at Pentecost; and we would not know the full significance of the return of the Lord Jesus Christ, that glorious hope that He has left for us. This Book tells us about these things. That is why I love it.

And then, as regards one's practical daily life, I find that there are many things written in this Book that God has put there for my learning and your learning, and I find that they are most extraordinarily appropriate to the needs of daily life. During the two years on Malta, many of the things written in this Book meant more to me than I can tell you, because they exactly met my needs. I read in this Book how God in the old times delivered those who put their trust in Him. I read how He saved His people from the hands of their enemies. I read these things, and I rejoiced in them because I knew that the God Who did these things in those days is still the same God today, and I proved it.

I used to revel in some of these wonderful stories, say about King Asa, when an enormous force of the enemy came against him, and God delivered him out of the hands of that superior force. I rejoice in reading that wonderful happening at Dothan when the prophet Elisha was there with his servant, and the servant got up early one morning, and to his dismay found that the city was beleaguered by a large force of the enemy. He did not know what to do; but I read that the prophet told him not to be afraid, for those who were with him were more than those who were against him.

Especially in the early days of the siege of Malta, when it seemed as if those who were with us were very few in number as compared with those of the enemy not very far away, God reminded me, through that story, and many others like it, that He can open our eyes so that we may see the horses and chariots of fire round about, just as Elisha prayed, and his servant's eyes were opened, and he saw them. One need not see these things with physical eyes; but I was just as sure as I could be that they were there, and that God's help was available, and He gave it, and I had never any doubt that He would give it from the beginning to the end.

One often hears that the Book which we are thinking about today is out of date, but it does not seem to me to be out of date. It met my needs in the years on Malta in a very special and wonderful way, and I like to realize that what this Book has been to me, it has been to many others all over the world in all sorts of circumstances. There is no circumstance too difficult but that God can meet our needs, by reminding us how He has dealt with and helped His servants in similar trials in olden days, and how He has done the same today. The Bible means all that to us; I hope it does — I am sure it does.

OUR GREAT HERITAGE
By Lady Dobbie
Written for *The Life of Faith,*
London

God has set up His standards for Christian living in the New Testament, in many chapters, but particularly in the Epistles (Rom. 12; Eph. 4 and 5; Phil. 2-4; Col. 3; I Thess. 5; Timothy and James). As we look through God's Word with this in view we find that these rules are very explicit and practical.

They are for God's children—those who have come to Him as sinners, claimed His atonement, and have begun to live a new life in Christ Jesus. This cannot be too strongly stressed, for "they that are in the flesh cannot please God." The unconverted who have not the Spirit of God in their hearts have no life in them. All the virtues they show have varying motives and do not come from the single desire to please Him.

We must honestly admit, however, that many who ignore God, and flout His Word, live very good lives, and are often most charming and attractive. We have all of us been puzzled by this, at times. I once heard a very good simile used to account for it. It was that of a gorgeously dressed Christmas tree and a small puny pot-plant. The one has no power in itself to produce anything, however lovely it may appear. Everything is tied on outside, and eventually the tree must decay. The plant, though insignificant in appearance, has life within, and given the necessary requirements—air, water, sunshine—it will develop into perfect beauty.

Therefore, in considering the standards set up in God's Word, and handed down to us from our forebears, we take for granted that they apply only to those who are His redeemed children and have grace given them to follow His guidance, from the heart. We Christians, in this country especially, have a great inheritance in the open Bible and also in the godly traditions received from earlier generations. We must go far back into history to find our most valuable heritages.

William Tyndale, in the reign of Henry VIII, translated the Bible into English, had it printed abroad and sent to England. His ambition, expressed in his own words, was "Ere I die, the boy who followeth the plough shall read the Scriptures in his own tongue." Tyndale was later burned at the stake. Through his devoted labours, and those of others like him, we can freely read the Word of God. Let us not neglect it!

We have also much to be thankful for in the Puritans' tradition. The standards they set became a memory and a thrust at the conscience of the depraved society of a later period. Their literature and hymns were very fine, and are an inspiration still.

Then Bunyan's "Pilgrim's Progress," said to be second only to the Bible as the best seller in the world, has been used to the blessing of millions up to the present day. Children were brought up on it, and many a child and many a grown-up person, has met Christ for the first time through its pages.

Later, in the middle of the eighteenth century, the revival under the Wesleys and Whitefield and the flood of hymns produced by them re-introduced the doctrine of Justification by Faith, which had been Luther's slogan two centuries earlier, but had been lost almost entirely behind the materialism of the eighteenth century. All this has provided a spiritual heritage which has played a great part in forming our national character, and making our nation great.

It is the fashion nowadays to pour contempt on all we have received from previous generations, especially that immediately preceding our own. People say that the virtues cultivated were hypocritical, and partook of the Christmas-tree-illumination order. But the standards were good, and it is for us to follow what was good in them.

Have we slipped from these ideals? To take one example —how about Sunday observance? In the recollection of older people, the Sunday of our childhood was a wonderful day, very, very different from the other six. It was a day of rest and peace for the whole houshold—servants, animals, and the family. There was a complete cessation of business and bothers. Every member of the family went to church, or some place of worship, and there was no entertaining or games.

To the unconverted, such a day spelt boredom in the extreme, and those who abuse it prove that they have no spiritual aspirations. We do not well to conform to their desires in breaking down the old conventions regarding Sunday. The late Bishop Taylor-Smith was fond of asking people how many years of Sundays they had had in their lives. At thirty years of age, we have had over four years of the days set apart for God. What a wonderful influence they have had, if they have really been set apart for God's worship and work.

Then, the family prayers of my childhood were an institution met with in almost every house in which one stayed. The gathering of every member of the house drew them all together spiritually. Prayers may take different forms, as, when in Malta, we had three minutes extempore prayer for our cause, in the drawing-room of the Palace, after late dinner, with the family, and our guests, if they cared to join.

Or they may take the form of the old-fashioned assembling of the family and servants together before or after breakfast. It can be wedged in at some time in the day, however busy the household. God does honor the committing of the members of a house to Him, and incidentally, it makes for unity and confidence among them. This practice is wiped out of England now, with very few exceptions. It is for us evangelical Christians to "strengthen the things that remain."

Then it seems to me that common honor and righteousness are not taught as they used to be. It was not considered funny and clever to cheat the Government, railway companies, and other public bodies. Truth was much more highly esteemed than it is now. I was frankly shocked at a gathering of young people, not so long ago, when we discussed what we all considered the most important moral qualities. I found they all put loyalty before truthfulness; and other, to me much less important qualities, were put ahead.

I realize, on the other hand, that there are many things in which we have improved enormously on previous generations. Our sympathy with the poor, the sick, the aged, the insane, and the oppressed, is incomparably ahead of theirs. But it seems to be regarded as everything. The loving of the Lord our God has gone almost entirely—and our Lord put the latter first. He called it the first and great commandment. Loving God teaches love to one's neighbor, but the loving of the neighbor seems, in many cases, to be quite independent of love to God. Both are essential.

The most important thing, of course, is the bearing of these practices upon everyday conduct and character. It must be admitted that they did produce a high quality of Christian life. Our nation owes more than we can ever estimate to the Christian standards which have made our countrymen trusted and respected throughout the world. But today we are witnessing a breakdown in conduct. Is the reason difficult to see?

One of the greatest means of strength to us as a nation in World War II was the knowledge that we were fighting for righteous principles. Our people recognized what was right, and were ready to defend it against the Nazi evil. But the tragedy is that, at such a time as this, moral standards should become so lax as to be alarming. We are living on our spiritual capital—and it is running out. The foundations of national righteousness are being undermined.

Now, I began by saying that Christian standards are for Christian people; but we are to be the salt of the earth. We can only be such, to our nation, as we maintain the highest standards of conduct and character. And for the development of these, we need the discipline of regular reading of the Bible, worthy observance of the Lord's Day, acknowledgment of the Lord in our family life, and a high regard for the principles of integrity and honor.

We have received a great heritage—not to do with as we like, but to pass on. We are custodians of this inheritance; we hold it in trust to pass on to others as it has been passed on to us. The greatest service we can possibly render our nation today is the influence of true Christian lives—setting up a standard once again which shall be an inspiration and challenge to all with whom we have dealings. In this way we best can serve our day and generation, proving ourselves worthy of our great inheritance and preserving that inheritance for future generations.

In all these matters, we need to orient ourselves from time to time with the Bible. That is actually the only standard. But certain it is, that if scriptural standards of conduct are to be maintained, our lives must bear them out—else other people will ridicule them, and rightly so. It is the old story, faith and works must go together. Let us try, most heartily, to live up to the great traditions we have received. We must acknowledge and value all we have learned from those who lived before us; but let us remember that rules and regulations so practised are valueless unless they come from the only motive worth anything—a deep and humble love to God.

THE UNCHANGING GOD

This article and the two which follow appeared in the *Sunday School Times* early in General Dobbie's tour.

We live in an age which prides itself on its progress. We think of the tremendous advances made in many directions and of the great changes that have been brought about in many departments of human life. We are apt to be so much obsessed by the contemplation of these changes and by our pride in them that we are too often unmindful of the factors which do not change. One of these factors is human nature, which in its characteristics and need is the same today as it ever was. The other is God, who "changeth not," but is "the same yesterday, and today, and forever." It is to the unchangeableness of God that I desire to direct the thoughts of my readers in this short article.

God has revealed Himself to us in two ways—by His written Word, the Holy Scriptures, and by His Incarnate Word, the Lord Jesus Christ. I desire to give my testimony, humble but very sincere, to the way God has made Himself known to me through these means.

When I found myself in the position of Governor and Commander-in-Chief of the Island of Malta in the early summer of 1940, I found myself confronted with new problems and strange difficulties. It was at the time when Italy joined in the war against the British Empire, and France had been forced to give in. The situation in Malta—both as regards its extreme isolation and great weakness of its garrison—was far from enviable. The nearest friendly territory was nearly a thousand miles away. Owing to the general situation no reinforcements could be expected for an indefinite period. The enemy's strength greatly outnumbered the tiny garrison available— and his intention to attack and overwhelm the island by sheer force of numbers was trumpeted abroad. That was the situation as it appeared to us in June, 1940.

But God has made provision for such needs. We were not the first to find ourselves in such a situation. Many others before us had been faced with similar problems, and records exist of the way they faced and overcame their difficulties. Many of these records are to be found in Holy Writ, and were included there primarily for the help of others like ourselves who followed after, and who would seek to know the secret of their success.

The Old Testament is full of these accounts, many of which described situations strangely similar to that which confronted us in Malta, in 1940. The fact that nearly three thousand years had passed since they happened mattered not at all. True, many circumstances had changed. The weapons used today are very different from those used by the enemies of Judah, but the basic factors have remained unchanged, that is, man's need and God's readiness and power to help.

We are told in the New Testament that these incidents have been included for our help—"Whatsoever things were written aforetime were written for our learning, that we through patience and comfort of the Scriptures might have hope" (Rom. 15:4) —and in Malta we certainly found that that was so. I gained much comfort and hope from the Holy Scriptures, as I read how God had helped and delivered His people over and over again when they were threatened or attacked by an enemy in apparently overwhelming strength: and I am sure many others in Malta were encouraged, too.

We realized that, although our human resources were woefully weak, we need not be anxious if Almighty God would help us. He is not on "the side of the strong battalions," as Napoleon cynically said. He can help "with many, or with them that have no power." We know what He did in the case of Gideon—how He used only three hundred men against the vast forces of the enemy. Little certainly is much, if God is in it.

I noticed also from the Scriptures that while God sometimes bids us stand aside and watch Him act, that is exceptional. Usually He has required His people to do their part to the full extent of their ability, but of course in reliance on Him. He does not act for us simply that we may sit back and take our ease. Nehemiah showed the right combination: "We made our prayer to God, and set a watch" (Neh. 4:9). We tried to act on that principle in Malta. We did all we could to insure the safety of the fortress, and at the same time we made our prayer to our God.

With these thoughts in our minds, it may be helpful to consider some of the Old Testament stories to which I have referred above.

Take the case of Elisha in Dothan as recorded in II Kings 6. We read that his servant in the early morning found to his dismay that the town was surrounded by a hostile army. He went to his master and said: "Alas, my master! how shall we do?" Elisha's reply was illuminating: "Fear not: for they that be with us are more than they that be with them." That was recorded for the comfort and hope of those that come after, including us in Malta. We can gratefully say that, although our physical eyes may not have seen the horses and chariots of fire round about Malta, yet the actual help and deliverance given us by God was very clearly in evidence—so much so that many were remarking upon it.

It is interesting to notice that Hezekiah the King some time later used a similar expresison to encourage the people of Jerusalem, as recorded in II Chronicles 32: 7, 8: "There be more with us than with him: with him is an arm of flesh; but with us is the Lord óur God to help us, and to fight our battles." No wonder we read that the people rested themselves upon the king's words. The New Testament version is found in Romans 8:31: "If God be for us, who can be against us?"

Jehoshaphat, another King of Judah, provides yet another instance. His country was threatened by a vast horde of the enemy. He was quite unable to put in the field any adequate force with which to repel them; but he prayed, just as we in Malta prayed, "We have no might against this great company . . . neither know we what to do: but our eyes are upon thee." God's answer to him may well be taken to heart by us: "Be not afraid . . . for the battle is not yours, but God's" (II Chron. 20).

That is just as much a fact in this twentieth century as it was at any time in the past. God has not changed. His power is no less than it was. It is infinite. His ear is just as open to the cry of need as it ever was, and prayer offered in the name of the Lord Jesus Christ is always heard by Him, and answered by Him in the way which He in His wisdom and love sees is best.

But there is another side to this question. While we may not doubt God's willingness and power to help, yet we must remember that He expects certain things from us. We have already seen that He expects us to do our part so far as we are able, but He expects more than that.

Joshua lifts the curtain and allows us to see. The people of Israel were about to cross the river Jordan and to invade Canaan. God promised His support and help so long as they walked in His way. Joshua then told the people what was expected of them. In the first place they were to make all the reasonable preparations which they could. "Prepare you victuals" (Josh. 1: 11), for the campaign which was to start in three days' time. Then two days later, he told them, "Tomorrow the Lord will do wonders among you" (3:5). But there was something more. Before God could do these wonders something more was needed. The people were told, "Sanctify yourselves."

We are too prone to expect God to do wonders among us, while we continue to lead lives that are far from sanctified. We like to remind ourselves of the righteousness of our cause, and it undoubtedly is righteous, but we are apt to overlook the fact that we are not righteous. We seem to think that God is willing to bring about His purposes of righteousness by means of instruments which are unrighteous, and perhaps deliberately so. We need to face up to this, both saint and sinner, and the saint needs to do it first.

We Christians have much for which to humble ourselves before God. We need to examine ourselves, and to ask God to search us and know our hearts, and see if there be any wicked way in us. Then and then only can He lead us in the way everlasting (Psa. 139:23, 24). Both nationally and individually this is needed if we are to expect God to help us in our times of difficulty. Again I would repeat that Christians must face up to this question, for then and then only will they be able to influence the nation to face it, and to bring forth fruits worthy of repentance.

God's help in battle raises many questions which cannot be dealt with here. It may be asked, for instance, what will happen if children of God in the ranks of our enemies are asking His help? God always answers prayer in the way which He sees best. He is working His purposes out, and He directs events to that end. But the object of the above thoughts is to show that God has not changed, that He does still interest Himself in the affairs of His creatures, that He does intervene in order to bring about the fulfillment of His purposes, that He does hear and answer the prayer of faith, and, in a word, that it is still no vain thing to trust in the living God, even in this materialistic twentieth century.

MAN'S UNCHANGING NEED

In the previous article we were considering the "Unchanging God" and were noticing how He still helps those who seek Him and trust Him, just as He has always done. In this article we shall consider another thing which is unchanging, and that is man's need.

We have made wonderful progress in scientific discovery since Bible days, and we have applied many of these discoveries to the amelioration of the human lot. In the field of medicine alone we have successfully grappled with problems caused by disease and have reduced the death rate in our cities, perhaps increasing the "expectation of life." In the field of communications astounding results have been achieved. We can travel from one place to another far more quickly, safely, and comfortably, than would have been thought possible 100 years ago. We can send messages with the speed of light to our friends at the other side of the world and can hear their actual voices speaking to us from thousands of miles away.

But in spite of all these and many other advantages, man is no happier today than he used to be; indeed as we look round upon the world with all its turmoil, distress, and unrest, we are forced to the conclusion that man is less happy than he was in other times and that this unhappiness is increasing rather than diminishing.

The fact is, of course, that all the wonderful discoveries and inventions only touch man on the physical and mental planes. They do not touch him on the spiritual plane at all; and it may be for that reason that many of these scientific discoveries have been used, not for man's well-being, but for his destruction. That, unfortunately, is a fact which cannot be gain-said, and which must be faced. Man's progress on the mental and physical planes may perhaps be very wonderful, but it is because his spiritual needs have been largely overlooked, or crowded out by the others, that the widespread misery exists today.

Man's spiritual needs are, in reality, the greatest and most important of all his needs. They cut deepest, and affect the foundation on which the superstructure of his whole life must be built. And this need of man is unchanged; it is exactly the same today as it was in the time of our first parents, and is caused by sin. Sin is an unpalatable fact, but it is a fact, as is surely very evident as we look into our own hearts. Facts must be faced, if we are to build a stable structure. It is unbelieveably foolish to act like the ostrich, which buries its head in the sand and thinks all must be well because it refuses to see danger.

Nowadays there is a tendency to refuse to recognize sin as sin. We call it by some other name. We tone it down and persuade ourselves that it does not really matter. We accept the devil's argument that "anyhow we are no worse than many others." We deliberately shut our eyes to what God thinks about sin, and to what He says about it. One might have thought that we would recognize the importance of finding out what God thinks about sin, since it is that which really matters. But in order that man may not find out what God says about sin, the devil has sought to undermine confidence in God's Word, the Holy Scriptures, with lamentable results. God's estimate of sin we see in the Cross. That was the price which had to be paid to release us from the penalty and power of sin —and no lesser price would suffice.

> "Oh, how vile my low estate,
> If my ransom was so great."

Sin in man is an unchanging fact, but, thank God, it is

a fact which may be faced with confidence since God has
provided a Remedy. Not only is man's need unchanging, but
the Remedy is unchanging as well. And the Remedy is just
as efficacious as it ever was. Moreover it is the only Remedy
—no other has been found which can effect the cure, nor is
any other accepted or recognized by God. It is a Remedy
that has never failed, as millions alive today and countless
millions who have lived can confidently attest. The writer of
this article is one, who by God's infinite grace, can "say so"
also.

In God's mercy to me, He brought me to know Him at an
early age. I was only 14 years old, a schoolboy at Charterhouse School. He first brought me to realize my need. He
showed me that I was a sinner, and that things were not
right between God and me. This knowledge was a heavy
burden on me, and made me a miserable person. I can now
thank God He did put that burden upon me, and that I felt
its weight, since otherwise I might never have sought relief,
nor found the Remedy. I had been brought up in a truly Christian family, and had heard the gospel message over and over
again. I knew it so well and it became so familiar to me, that its
real meaning did not come home to me; but the great burden
that God in His mercy put upon me brought me to seek
relief. It was the Holy Spirit "convincing me of my sin," and
He brought me to face up to my state and my need.

I shall not forget my relief when I realized that Christ
had died for me. I was carrying a heavy burden from which
I longed to be freed, and I suddenly saw that it was precisely
for the purpose of freeing me from that burden that the
Lord Jesus Christ had come to the earth and had given His
life. I saw that He had taken my place, had paid the infinite
debt I had incurred, had settled it once and for all, and was
offering to me complete liberation from the penalty of sin.
When I realized this, I then and there accepted Him as my

Saviour on these terms, namely, that He had done all that was necessary when He gave His life for me, and I had only to accept this wonderful gift.

That transaction between Him and me took place many years ago, and in all the intervening period I have never been able to doubt that it was a real thing which happened then, and that God, the holy and righteous God, for Christ's sake forgave me my many sins.

But man's need goes even further than that. Deliverance from the penalty of sin must be the first thing, since only thus can one become a "child of God through faith in Jesus Christ." But man also needs deliverance from the power of sin. This is necessary because a child of God must be able to glorify Him in his life down here. It is by this that men can judge of the reality of the change which comes to us at the new birth. They cannot see into our hearts, nor know what has passed between us and God; but they can see our lives, and if they see that sin apparently has just as much power in our lives as before, they are entitled to doubt the reality of the change which we profess. "By their fruits ye shall know them."

But, thank God, Christ meets this need, too. When we accept Him as Saviour from the penalty of sin, He does not leave us there. He does not tell us to go along as best we can— far from it. He says to us: "Now that I have come into your life, I am not going to leave you; we will from henceforth go together. The path of your life will be beset with dangers; there will be enemies lying in wait for you, and trying to trip you up. If I am with you, you need not fear them, but without Me you can do nothing. I have a special interest in you in view of the price I paid for your redemption. Moreover your life may easily dishonor My Father, unless I hold you up. So, 'I will never leave you nor forsake you,' and I will be with you unto the very end. But watch carefully lest you allow anything to come into your life which will prevent Me from helping you. I will garrison your heart if you will let Me. If you open the door I will come in and live with you and in you."

Here is the absolute answer to all our need. He has promised that "sin shall not have dominion over you," and He is always ready to substantiate that promise. But it must be He who does it; we have not the power ourselves apart from Him.

I wonder if we realize how important it is that our lives should be holy and victorious. On them depends the value of our testimony. We are left here to be His witnesses, and, to a large extent, all that the world knows of Him and of God is what they see in us. We need constantly to be on the watch that we let the world see Christ in us, as He really is. It is one of the chief aims of the devil to make Christians show by their lives a distorted view of Christ. Such a view will never attract others to Him; rather will it repel them.

May God give us grace to be careful in this all-important matter so that no one will be repelled from Christ on account of what he may see in us. The only way of avoiding such a terrible thing is by handing oneself over to His keeping and allowing His Holy Spirit to dwell in us and fill us. Let us "walk humbly with . . . God," and then we shall "walk honestly toward them that are without." He has promised that He is able to keep us from falling (or even stumbling), but it takes His strong right arm to do this.

Finally, let us be diligent in this matter. We cannot overrate the importance of it. God chooses to work through human instruments, but these must be clean and fit for the Master's use. God is willing to do His part, but He calls upon us to do ours, and to be in dead earnest about it. We need to be in constant touch with Him through prayer and the study of the Scriptures. We need to ask Him to search us "and see if there be any wicked way in" us. We need to examine ourselves in the searchlight of His Word, and anything that He shows us is displeasing to Him, we must be willing ruthlessly to put away.

THE UNCHANGING FOUNDATION

In Great Britain (and probably in the United States as well) the word "reconstruction" is on many persons' lips, and a great deal of thought is being given to this all-important matter. The long years of war have brought in their train an upheaval and a dislocation which has shaken our nations to their core. Many cherished illusions have been shattered; we gaze upon much desolation, both physical and moral; and we peer into the future and wonder how a new and better order of things can be produced out of all this chaos.

As we consider the future, we must not lose sight of the lessons of the past. These surely have been clear and definite; we have undoubtedly heard God's voice speaking to us both nationally and individually, and we have seen His actions, as He has sought to teach us the lessons we so greatly need to learn. We have been reminded in a forcible way that God both brings us down and lifts us up. He has both humbled us and delivered us. We have seen that His help is the one thing that matters most, and have surely learned that He, and He alone, is the Giver of victory. In making our plans for the future, we msut therefore insure that these things, some of which have been learned in the hard school of suffering, are not forgotten, and that God has His right place in all our future plans.

In constructing (or indeed reconstructing) any edifice, there is a proper order for the various processes which are needed. No man in his senses would dream of departing from this order in the material realm, thought it is to be feared that some are disposed to do so in the spiritual sphere.

The first thing that must be seen to and insured is not the superstructure, but the foundation. However beautiful the former may be, it cannot last unless the latter is " well and truly laid." Of course, the foundation is usually out of sight, and for that reason is apt to be out mind; but, for all that, it is without exception the most important part of the building, since upon it all the other parts depend.

Our Lord recognized the importance of this truth, and warned His disciples against any disregard of it. His parable of the two foundations recorded in Mathew 7 and in Luke 6 should be carefully studied by all of us. The vital difference between the two houses lay only in the foundations; the superstructures may have been identical, in fact, the house built on the sand may have been the more attractive of the two in its outward appearance. But the importance of the unseen foundation became evident as soon as the testing time came. In one case the house not only did not fall, but was not even shaken (Luke 6:48). In the other case "it fell; and great was the fall of it."

In our plans for reconstruction, whether of our national life or of our individual lives, may we remember that the foundation is what matters. Whatever else we do or leave undone, let us insure, as thank God we may, that the foundation is right. Then, and only then will we be able to build an edifice that will serve the purpose we desire, and which God desires. Then, and only then, will we be sure that it cannot be shaken or destroyed. Then, and only then, will we be able to face the unknown future, with its difficulties and trials, with absolute confidence.

And what is this sure foundation on which we must build? We saw earlier in this article that we must insure that God take His rightful place in our plans. He is the foundation on whom we must build. We have surely learned in the hard school of war that we cannot do without Him, and must remember that just as we need Him in war, so do our nations need Him in peace. The plans which we make must be built on Him, His will, and His Word. We must be prepared to face the issue as we ask Him to indicate to us His will.

This may involve many adjustments in our national lives. It may involve a reorientation of our attitude to certain things which we know are displeasing to Him. His law will have to displace many of our cherished ideas. He will have to be first in our national life. Well will it be with our nations if that end is achieved. David described such a state of affairs in these words, "Happy is that people, whose God is the Lord" (Psa. 144:15). Moses' version was as follows, "Happy art thou, O Israel: who is like unto thee, O people saved by the Lord, the shield of thy help, and who is the sword of thy excellency!" (Deut. 33:29). This may be the experience of any nation that really puts God in His rightful place.

But there is a danger that in considering what the nation should do, we overlook something which is even more important still, and that is our attitude as individuals to this vital matter. It is one thing to long for our nation to be rebuilt on the right foundation, but it is another thing to insure that we ourselves are! And yet the nation will never get right unless and until we individuals get right first.

Our Lord in the parable we have been considering likened the good foundation to a rock. That is, moreover, a picture used in Scripture of the Lord Himself. He is the Rock, the Rock Christ Jesus, the Rock of Ages. We individuals need to make sure that we are building on Him, and not on the shifting sands of our own efforts and imagined righteousness. Only as we are on that firm ground ourselves will we be able to help others on to it, too. We cannot hope to drag any one out of a bog, if we are in it ourselves. We must first have our "goings established," before we can help others.

David describes this process very clearly in Psalm 40: "He

brought me up also out of an horrible pit, out of the miry clay, and set my feet upon a rock, and established my goings." Then we notice the sequel: "A new song in my mouth . . . many shall see it, and fear, and shall trust in the Lord." That is the right, in fact, the only possible sequence. By that way and that alone can we become the instrument in God's hands of helping others on to the firm foundation, for which so many seem to be seeking in vain.

In Malta, during the siege, we were constantly being reminded of this great truth by means of the rock of which the island mainly consists. It gave us sure foundations on which to build the various defensive works we needed; foundations that would not shift and could not be shaken by enemy bombs, or by the discharge of our own guns.

But the rock of Malta was a blessing to us for other reasons as well. Not only could we build upon it; we were able also to dig into it, and so provide for the people shelter accommodation which was entire proof against the worst that the enemy could do. Those abiding in these rock shelters were entirely safe, and knew it! However great was the din outside, however widespread the havoc outside, those within could lay them down in peace and sleep, without one vestige of anxiety for their own personal safety, or for that of their loved ones who were in the shelter with them. If only Toplady could have lived in the siege of Malta, he would have realized how wonderfully fitting were the words of his hymn:

> "Rock of Ages, cleft for me;
> Let me hide myself in Thee."

It is with their spiritual meaning that we are now concerned. Let us review afresh our relationship with the Lord Jesus Christ, the Rock whom God has provided for us. Have we laid our foundation upon Him and His finished work? Are we really sheltering in that Rock which was cleft for us, when He made atonement for sin by the sacrifice of Himself? Do we realize that all the storm of God's just wrath for our sins fell upon Him, so that none need fall upon us? And are we really grateful to Him for having done all this for us? As we answer these questions before God, we will long that others of our nation (and other nations, too) may enter into this same peace and security, and we will then be in a position to help them to it, as we tell them of what we know, or rather, of the One whom we know.

We long for national revival: it must begin in us who name the name of Christ. There is much in us that needs to be put right before we can influence others and lead them to our God and Saviour. We need to examine ourselves so as to insure that nothing in us is hindering the work of God in our land. Let us give over examining each other, and let us concentrate on ourselves. Let us humble ourselves before Almighty God, and ask Him to "search me, O God, and know my heart: try me, and know my thoughts. And see if there be any wicked way in me, and lead me in the way everlasting" (Psa. 139:23, 24).

That is the beginning of our contribution to the reconstruction of our nation. We know that Christ is the solution for all the troubles and difficulties of the nation, and of all the individuals who compose it. We have got to get this fact across to them in such a way that, not only will they understand it, but will also be convinced by it. We have to present Christ to them, not only by lip, but even more by life. We have to speak with assurance of what we know of Him; firsthand evidence is required.

But we must show Him to them in our lives, so that we convince them by what we show to them as well as by what we say to them. We need to convince them, both that they need Him, and that He can satisfy their need. We must do this humbly but confidently, and in His power. He has left us here to be witnesses to Him; that is our *raison d'être*. May

He keep us constantly alive to this great fact, and may He enable us so to live as to attract others to Him.

When our Lord was leaving Gadara, the man whom He had healed desired to go with Him. Our Lord said, No. "Go home to thy friends, and tell them (show, in Luke 8:39) how great things the Lord hath done for thee" (Mark 5:19). And so He says to us. May we have grace to obey His commands.